The 10x Growth Machine

How companies can innovate, scale and win

Misha de Sterke

Boom | Management IMPACT

Dear Sara!

Hope this book provide you some new perspectives and insights. Looking forward to a collaboration.

Best regards

Misha

TABLE OF CONTENTS

Warning   **11**

Foreword by Peter van Grinsven   **15**

Chapter 1
Corporate innovation – an introduction   **19**
1.1   Creative destruction is accelerating   19
1.2   The growth paradox and need for continuous innovation   22
1.3   Corporate innovation challenges   24
1.4   Why continuous innovation is hard for corporations   25

Chapter 2
The 10x Growth Machine system   **35**

2.1   10x Growth Machine building blocks   39
2.2   10x Growth Machine principles – in pursuit of excellence   47
2.3   10x Growth Machine Canvas   51

Chapter 3
Growth Strategy and Portfolio management   **59**

3.1   Disruption and understanding the periphery   60
3.2   Growth Portfolio management – The link between strategy
      and execution   69
3.3   Venture boards – Think and act as an investor   77
3.4   Metered funding   85
3.5   Resource allocation process   95

Chapter 4
Corporate Venture Building   **99**

4.1   What problem should corporate venture building solve?   101
4.2   Way of working: Connect disruptive strategy with
      Lean Startup and Growth Hacking   103
4.3   The startup journey   105
4.4   End-to-end innovation process   107

Chapter 5
Growth Accounting   **125**

5.1   How Growth Accounting works   127
5.2   When you don't use innovation accounting   129
5.3   Metrics   130
5.4   Traps of measuring innovation   136

Chapter 6
Innovation management
141

6.1   Corporate startups, a two- front war   142
6.2   Organizing the intrapreneurship function   144
6.3   Two sets of rules and policies   150
6.4   Managing the startup to scale-up process   152
6.5   Pathways to business model discovery and validation   154

Chapter 7
Transformation for growth
163

7.1   Phase one: Art of the Start – build first success,
       learn how it works and create allies   164
7.2   Phase two: Governance – implement system building blocks,
       engage the organization   171
7.3   Phase three: Scale – perfect the practice,
       build A-teams within the organization   174

Afterword
Envisioning a Future-Proof organization
179

Notes   185
Literature   189
About the Author   191

Tools and checklists

10x Growth Machine Framework

10x Growth Machine Canvas

Corporate venture methodology

Guide to determine growth opportunity areas

Metric board for Growth Accounting

Innovation capability assessment

Portfolio Tool

Growth Transformation canvas

Disruption analysis checklist

Questionnaire: Determine the organization of the corporate entrepreneurship function

Corporate Startup Maturity – metered funding

Corporate Startup Maturity Level

Disruptive strategy checklist for venture boards

Checklist Innovation Director: Is your board onboard?

Evaluation of the Growth Machine

Evaluate the quality of your current strategy process

All tools are available at www.10xgrowthmachine.com

Warning

This book might well have had a different title, *In Pursuit of Excellence*. The problem with innovation is that for some people it can have negative connotations. It is perceived as creative people burning cash in cool places without being accountable for it. Unfortunately, this is true in some cases. Consultants and guru's selling illusions, the next methodology and framework (just like myself) or the next hype. These methodologies suggest that if you follow the steps, success will be the automatic result. But like any other top accomplishment in music, sport or business, there is no quick fix. Mastery and virtuosity require hard work, discipline and building the right mental muscle. Creating long-term growth for an established company successfully is an act of virtuosity. The reality is that most companies fail at it because it's difficult and complicated. Why do you think the top 20 list of the Fortune 500 has changed so dramatically in the last couple of years?

To build the Growth Machine requires, besides competence, curiosity and determination, also the emotional willpower to fight for this challenge without giving up in the process. To perform at this level, we need to develop and nourish the kind of habits of thinking, being and doing that lead to excellence. In this book, I'm offering a comprehensive framework, methodology and toolset that serves as a navigation map for you as an innovator, for understanding how to create new growth from non-incremental innovation. This methodology in itself will not guarantee success. That depends on how well you, as a reader, grasp the meaning of what I'm saying and then implement this perfectly in your company. This journey will transform you personally and, I hope, transform your company into becoming the best version of itself. Many companies have done this before. Think of all the old companies that still exist, like Nintendo, GKN, P&G, Fujitsu, IBM and many more.

I wish you all the best in the journey, a lot of emotional stamina and intellectual horsepower.

Misha de Sterke

For Viktoriya, Isabel, Nicholas & Mia

You remind me every day what matters most

Foreword

BY PETER VAN GRINSVEN

Most companies struggle with implementing a successful innovation strategy to create new business models and, thereby, new business. They witness startups and scale-ups disrupting their markets on the one hand, and on the other they struggle to break through their own bureaucratic and outdated ways of working and reporting. Only a few of the well-known companies have managed to create a future-proof *new* organization.

This remarkable book gives the reader some insight into how to crack the nut of creating a corporate Growth Machine by using innovation as a means, not as a goal in itself. Misha de Sterke presents a clear overview in which he shows a proven methodology. And pragmatic insights into how corporates could build new business models and create new ways of working, to implement innovation at the heart of their business.

The main reason I consider De Sterke's book to be a *must-read*, is that it clearly shows that, to become an innovative company, you need to be able to transform your organization and business models. That means thinking of innovation as a means, instead of a goal. It's not the model that is the critical element, nor new technologies. It is how colleagues, co-workers and management deal with them; it is indeed a 'people' business. It's the CEO that embraces this new way of thinking and working with the whole organization, and it's the senior management that understands the impact of controlling the company. The adjacent units (HR, Legal, Procurement) cooperate in a new fashion with the internal startups and the business units and start working in fresh innovative ways with the aforementioned models and technologies.

I congratulate Misha with his book, since it is the first book that I know of, that offers a clear overarching model to companies wishing to remain relevant in disruptive times, by combining great models, theories and provocative thinking with proven ways of working and pragmatic solutions.

And on a personal note, I thank him for being a crucial member of our ecosystem and a great colleague, who keeps pushing us to stay ahead of the innovation game.

Peter van Grinsven

CEO NL Startupbootcamp/Innoleaps/Talent Institute

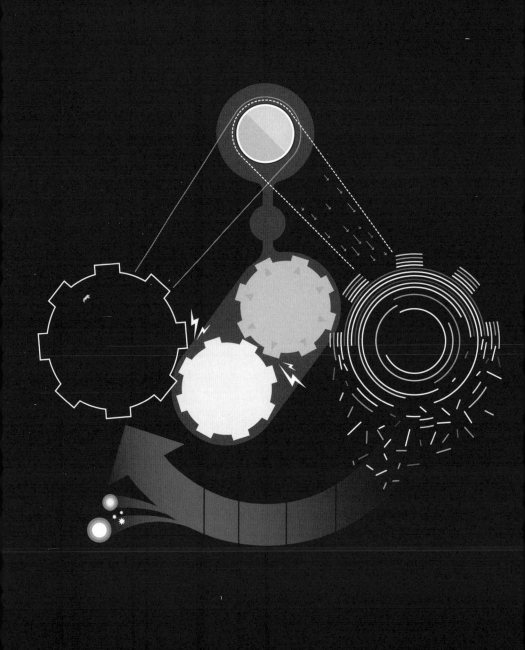

Chapter 1
Corporate innovation –
an introduction

Does your company have the right strategy to achieve growth? Is there an obsessive focus on the customers and the growth opportunities that they present?

1.1   Creative destruction is accelerating

Markets change, companies need to reinvent themselves. Their profit-oriented structure is designed to embrace the status quo. At the same time, the pace of creative destruction is accelerating.

Much of the talk about change seems to suggest that merrily rearranging things is enough. Leaders do not simply rearrange things. Leaders envision and create the future. A realistic life expectancy for a corporation is somewhere between 200 and 300 years. The average European corporation reaches 4% of its potential, while large corporations (> 10,000 employees or 5 billion market capitalization) reach 16%[1]. In terms of longevity, companies have a lot to gain. The average life expectancy for European and Japanese companies is 12.5 years and around 10% of all companies disappear each year. The logic of creative destruction is that new entrants arrive and incumbents disappear, but FASTER THAN EVER. The year-to-year viability of a company depends on its ability to innovate and create new waves of growth. Given today's market expectations, global competitive pressures and the extent and pace of structural change, that fact is truer than ever. Corporate lifespan is shrinking. Different pieces of longevity research share the same conclusions:

- Record private equity activity, a robust M&A market, and the growth of startups with billion-dollar valuations, are leading indicators of future turbulence.
- At the current churn rate, about half of S&P 500 companies will be replaced over the next ten years[2].
- Retailers were especially hit hard by disruptive forces and there are strong signs of restructuring in financial services, healthcare, energy, travel and real estate.
- From a recent benchmark study[3] among 270 innovation, strategy and R&D executives, focus shifts in the resource allocation process when it comes to innovation. The ratio of efforts dedicated to Optimize the Core, Renew the Core, and Future Growth, shifted to 50-30-20. The largest companies ($50B in revenue and up) spend even more energy on transformational work, 25%.

Chief executives struggle to make the case that their managerial actions can be reliable to yield a stream of successful new offerings. Typically, they are aware of a tremendous amount of innovation taking place in their enterprises, considering that large corporates invest between 2% and 10% from their topline in R&D. However, they don't feel that they have a grasp on all the dispersed initiatives. What is the success rate of R&D patents into new revenue models? The pursuit of the new feels episodic and executives suspect that the returns on the company's total innovation investment are too low. In my experience, what happens is that executives tend to respond with dramatic interventions and strategies.

To achieve top line growth, established companies need to change the way they operate. Consider that the top 50 consumer-goods manufacturers account for nearly 60% of industry sales, yet capture a mere 2% of its growth[4]. CEO's at these companies are nervous about their prospects and concerned about their business models, as they should be. Harvard Business School concludes that each year more than 30,000 new consumer products are launched and 80% of them fail. New waves of growth are hard to achieve.

My methodology is: being innovative pays off. Companies that are marketing and sales innovators are growing at 4.1% faster, when compared to companies[5] lagging behind in this field. However, in the last several years, incumbent CPG's (consumer packaging goods) have struggled to keep up with startups, which have reinvigorated and reinvented categories, ranging from ice cream to diapers. 30 years ago, almost half of the 100 largest companies on the New York Stock Exchange that enjoyed strong shareholders returns but did not post top-line growth, had been acquired or delisted 20 years later. Despite all these numbers, I see that many companies continue to focus on controlling costs as a way to drive earnings. When costs cutting dominates the corporate agenda, it sucks the oxygen out of any growth plan.

Kraft Heinz

Over the past few years, Brazilian investment firm 3G has deployed brutal cost-cutting to raise profits at Anheuser-Busch InBev, Burger King and **Kraft Heinz***, using an approach called zero-based budgeting. It requires that each expense is justified from scratch each year, as opposed to the traditional approach of adding a couple of percentage points to last year's line items. The strong implication is that managers should strive to lower all costs from one period to the next, at all costs. A Harvard Business School article in 2016 warned that the technique is "not a wonder diet for companies." That prophecy was confirmed by Kraft Heinz* **catastrophic announcement** *that stock price plunged by 20%.* [6]

Kraft Heinz desperately needs new products, but that can only be achieved by targeted spending on R&D, marketing and creative thinking. Conversely, companies that systematically pursue a clear agenda for organic growth outperform the competition.

Why is it so difficult for established companies to achieve corporate growth?

1.2   The growth paradox and need for continuous innovation

Innovation is the driver of growth and prosperity, though not every innovation is equal and not all types of innovation create new growth, as the Kraft Heinz case tells us. New growth comes from new-market innovations – that is *disruptive innovation*. Disruptive innovation makes products accessible and cheaper for everybody and creates new market growth. Think about how the T-Ford created an entire new market by making cars accessible to the mass market. On the other hand, we have *sustaining innovation*, which makes existing products better. The evolution of the television screen went from plasma to HD-ready, to Full HD, to 4K, to 8K, etc. It is advanced technology, but is used in the same product category. Sustaining innovation plays an important role, they improve margins, create bigger market share, but they don't create new growth in the longer term. Another type of innovation is called *efficiency innovation*. The purpose of this is to make more with less. This is equally important, because a company that does not get more efficient will probably perish. By its very nature, efficiency innovation kills jobs and Kraft Heinz was focused solely on efficiency innovation. They eliminated jobs and created free cash flow. But where did the money go? The reality shows us that there is no connection between freeing up cash and investing in disruptive innovation. It leads to the dynamic of investing in cost-cutting operations and, when that is successful, continuing that path.

The title of this book, *The 10x Growth Machine*, is straightforward: to create new growth, corporations should focus on new-market/disruptive innovations. It is the only way for established companies to stay future-proof. Established companies are structured to make money with their current business model and internally aligned (processes, people, metrics etc.) to perform that task. It is this alignment that prevents them from selecting and growing (disruptive) innovations. This is the heart of the growth dilemma that established companies face today.

This book provides an integrated set of building blocks, principles and tools to create different innovations as a structural way of working. Not by luck or heroism, but by building a Growth Machine that systematically ideates, validates and scales new business models, all brought together in the 10x Growth Machine Methodology.

The 10x Growth Machine Methodology is a battle-tested and integral approach for corporations to manage the startup to scaling-up process in a corporate setting. It enables corporates to create a Growth Machine that co-exists with the mother organization, thus finding a balance between executing the business and inventing future business. It is the change management approach for corporates that have innovation as a top priority and want to cope with the accelerated pace of creative destruction in the markets they operate in. The big idea is to build a second operating system (the Growth Machine), beside the "mothership", facilitating a discovery-driven entrepreneurial way of working, embedded in a system of processes, metrics and the leadership that nourishes it. Building this system, carefully managing the capabilities and the integration pathways of new business and its people towards the existing organization, is the key to successful 'scaling-up'.

New growth ventures need to be managed proactively and continuously, instead of trying to find new ventures only when the portfolio dries up. As the previous example shows, most companies know they need to innovate but have not yet learned to do this continuously and strategically. Companies that have the strongest innovation track record can articulate a clear innovation ambition and they have struck the right balance in *Optimizing the Core*, *Renewing the Core* and *Future Growth* initiatives across the enterprise. They have put tools and capabilities in place to manage those various initiatives as part of an integrated whole. To deal with this challenge, we need people who can practice the leadership that deals with all the tensions that innovation brings. We need to understand that the organizational designs and most employees working in them, are not equipped to innovate on these three playing fields.

A European consumer goods company, attuned to the need to keep its brands fresh in retailers' and consumers' minds, introduced frequent improvements and variations on its core offerings. Most of those earned their keep with respectable uptake by the market and decent margins. Over time, it became clear that all this product proliferation (splitting the revenue pie into ever-smaller slices) wasn't actually growing the pie. Eager to achieve a higher return, management launched a strategy aimed at breakthrough product development – at transformational rather than sustaining innovations. Unfortunately, this company's structure and processes were not set up to execute that ambition, although it did have the requisite capabilities for envisioning, developing and market testing innovations close to its core. It neither recognized, nor gained the very different capabilities needed to take a bolder path. Its most innovative ideas ended up being diluted beyond recognition, killed outright or crushed under the weight of the enterprise. Before long, the company retreated to what it knew best. Little was ventured and less was gained – and this cycle repeated itself.

1.3   Corporate innovation challenges

Based on my corporate innovation work with public and private companies – exchanging knowledge with peers and researching the topic of corporate innovation – it is good to share insights on the challenges established companies are facing, when it comes to corporate innovation. Let's start with a paradox. Good management is probably the number one reason companies like Kodak failed to stay on top of their game. They did everything right, created focus groups to listen to customers, invested in R&D to create better performing products, analyzed market trends and invested in innovations that promised the best return on investment. *Still* they lost their market leader position.

At top universities we are taught to create business models based on high profits and low-cost structures for our best customers. This perspective holds ground when it comes to improving existing business in known markets. Then it is important to invest in new technology and create better products for a higher margin. But when it comes to building new growth

Keep your eye on what drives the bottom-line, then develop those capabilities and the numbers will always meet or exceed your expectations[8].

As in the case of Sterling Drug, the dominant cultural pattern manifests itself in three fears[9]: fear of cannibalization of an important product line, the fear of channel conflict with important customers and the fear of dilution that might result from strategic acquisition. As reasonable as these fears seem to be for established companies, they are not felt in the market, so the market moves where the corporation dares not go.

A global FMCG company wants to play in the Brazilian market. In order to do so, they acquire the second biggest company in the market. The Brazilian market is very different in comparison with other markets, where the company had already been operating, as well as the margins. Due to the different markets and margins, the overall top line growth becomes diluted, initiating an internal discussion. If growth numbers are diluting, the likelihood of the capital markets providing investment money declines. Was it wise to acquire this company in a different market? They are now the second player in one of the largest economies.

I've been in organizations where the management meeting was the place where the CEO approved or disapproved proposals for senior management, prepared by a heavily centralized budget and planning department. If planning approved this, the CEO would sign off. If the CEO felt differently, he would disapprove the proposal without allowing the argument to be reviewed by the planning and budgeting department; senior management was waiting for their proposals to be hammered. I have also been in management meetings of fourteen people, where nobody made decisions, because everybody was waiting for the support of the others. And nobody wanted to take responsibility due to dramatic cost-cutting interventions in the past. Other senior management meetings were not about strategy and tactics at all, but only about who made which deals, for which numbers.

This kind of managerial stalemate is the source of most of the long-term lack of competitiveness one sees in corporations. The market has a better dialogue, thousands of 'buy and sell' conversations happen every day. New products and services are embraced; others are discarded within the blink of an eye.

The good part is that many companies have embraced Lean Startup or other forms of discovery-driven planning. The Lean Startup is a revolutionary methodology which provides the right kind of mindset and the tools to fast learning, through experimentation by rapid launching of MVP's (*Minimum Viable Products*) in the market. It is the only quick way to figure out if and how you need to build products that consumers want. Corporations start to embrace this technique; external agencies are hired to coach teams, bringing templates, tools and processes to go from an idea to a validated business model.

But in which cases does this really lead to new growth for the corporate? Does it really move the needle?

An interesting example is IBM. Over a 20-year period IBM went from success to failure to success. They transformed from a technology company, to a broad-based solutions provider, to an exemplar of open systems and on-demand possibilities. In the 1990's IBM's stock price was the lowest since 1983 and by 1992 more than 60,000 jobs were lost. Back in 1993, when Lou Gerstner took over, the services unit was 27% of revenues and the software service unit did not exist. By 2001, services and software were $35 billion and $13 billion businesses respectively and the share price had increased seven times. What happened? IBM had leveraged its intellectual capital and resources into business as diverse as life sciences, automotive and banking.

As Gerstner observed: "What happened to this company was not an act of God. People took our business away".

The company didn't lack smart people or winning strategies from consultancy firms, the problem was that the company was frozen in place, consistently missing the emergence of new industries. First, they lost the commercial router to Cisco, next they lost speed recognition software to Nuance, and Akamai won the market for internet performance software. What IBM lacked was not the ability to foresee threats and opportunities, but the capability to reallocate assets and reconfigure the organization to address them. IBM had great process managers, but you cannot institutionalize success in processes, because they are designed to execute, stabilize and scale production. The challenge for IBM was how to focus and remain agile.

Tushman and O'Reilly[10] give five major reasons for the failure of IBM:

1. Management system rewarded execution at short-term results, so the cost structure and financial performance of the organization made sure nothing changed. IBM was driven by process and did not value strategic business building.
2. The company was preoccupied with current markets and existing offerings. The logic behind this is financial for two reasons. The first reason is that with current markets we know how to size the market and make our efforts accountable, according to traditional accounting metrics like ROI, RONA, etc. The second reason is simple: most companies make the best profit margins with their existing offerings.
3. The business model emphasized sustained profits and earnings rather than actions towards higher prices and earnings.
4. The approach IBM used for gathering and using market insights was inadequate for new markets, and the insistence on fact-based financial analysis hindered the ability to generate market intelligence for new and ambiguous markets.
5. IBM lacked disciplines for selecting, experimenting, funding and terminating new growth. Leaders applied mature business processes to growth opportunities; as a result they often starved new ventures.

The paradox of the IBM success and failure history is that the alignment that made the company a disciplined machine, competing in mature business, was directly opposed to what they needed to be successful in emerging markets. In Chapter 2, The 10x Growth Machine system, I explain how to setup a growth-oriented governance system that facilitates innovation.

Points to ponder

It must be clear that going on innovation trips to Silicon Valley, organizing innovation tournaments, running sprints and accelerators are great fun, but they do not move things forward on their own. A system that enables and incentivizes fast learning and entrepreneurship should be embedded in the company. Real innovation impact requires real resources, just like your Marketing and Finance departments need real resources.

Given the non-deterministic nature of innovation, investing money in scaling a venture, unfortunately, does not happen systematically and with the right execution. The lack of connection between the innovation teams and their parent organization, which leads to dried up (corporate) startups, isn't due to funding but lack of resources. The initial funding between 50k–150k is not the problem, but the funds needed to scale-up the business are substantial and require top management sign-off. If we leave the process of resource allocation function on default, we definitely know that resources will be drawn to core business activities and sustaining innovations, because that is where the money is being made now. As a result, there is no way to finish and deploy whatever innovative prototypes the entrepreneurs have developed, even those that have been validated. In many corporations, there is no end-to-end innovation process and no effective decision-making infrastructure for the allocation of resources. Innovation teams don't have the mandate nor the people to build the type of end-to-end innovation pipeline process that goes from sourcing ideas, all the way to integrating their prototypes into mainstream production. Ideas that are implemented are small and scaled too carefully to create a sizable impact. Additionally, in the resource allocation process, management often fails to put their best people or sufficient resources into these activities. Startups in this stage easily get a 5 million to 10 million budget from investors, whereas a corporate startup rarely gets a 7-figure budget altogether.

This leads to the next challenge, how do we use and re-allocate the assets of the corporate to build new growth engines? And how do we make sure that what the teams learn from the market, will inform our corporate strategy on a quarterly base, instead of a three-year plan?

Make sure that strong innovation concepts, those that satisfy customer desirability and commercial viability, are properly integrated in the formal organization.

Should a venture be entirely separated from the core business as a stand-alone venture? Should it be integrated into an existing business unit? Or should it balance separation and integration by implementing an ambidextrous organizational setup? In many organizations, no appropriate guidelines for this have been issued up till now, although this poses a necessary condition for dual innovation success[11].

I witness teams going back to their own organization in a state of alienation, while at the same time existing priorities take precedence. They speak a foreign language (talking about MVP's, pivots and other startup slang) to their colleagues and superiors, who are rewarded on execution-based metrics, like return on investment or discounted cashflow. There is no metric system in corporations for translating what innovation teams have learned, into the kind of slang and metrics accountants prefer.

The 10x Growth Machine Methodology deals with these issues and shows how a company can create a system, the *Growth Machine*, with the right checks and balances and processes to churn out new growth engines in a systematic way. In the next chapter I will present the framework, methodology and building blocks necessary to build the corporate Growth Machine. In Chapter 3 we talk about how to pursue growth, where this growth comes from and whether we can relate the identified 'growth domains' for the company to an innovation portfolio with 50 relevant projects. Chapter 4 is about *corporate venture building,* in which we explain how we can build commercially viable ventures in the corporation and start executing on the portfolio. Chapter 5 is about measurements: how do we measure and track the progress of our early or later stage innovations? Chapter 6 deals

with the management aspect of corporate innovation and entrepreneurship. The core question is: how do we govern the Growth Machine in a way
that intrapreneurship can flourish? Chapter 7 brings all the previous chapters together and merges them into a pragmatic change management approach on how to scale this way of thinking and working in an established
company.

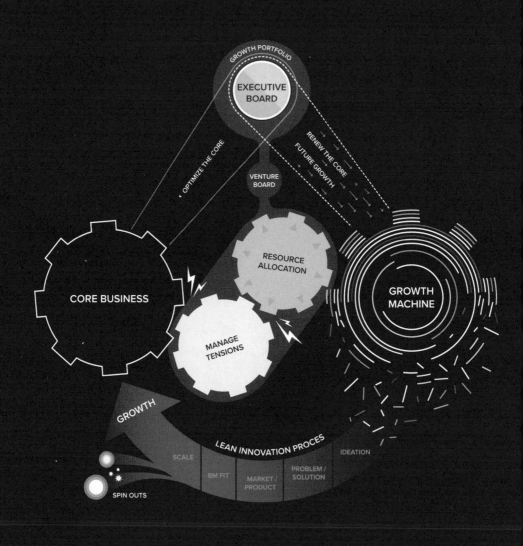

GROWTH PORTFOLIO

EXECUTIVE
BOARD

OPTIMIZE THE CORE

RENEW THE CORE

FUTURE GROWTH

VENTURE
BOARD

RESOURCE
ALLOCATION

CORE BUSINESS

MANAGE
TENSIONS

GROWTH
MACHINE

GROWTH

LEAN INNOVATION PROCES

SCALE

BM FIT

MARKET /
PRODUCT

PROBLEM /
SOLUTION

IDEATION

SPIN OUTS

Chapter 2
The 10x Growth Machine system

Corporate innovation is not about managing an unconnected set of tools, such as incubators, accelerators, startup engagement programs, intrapreneurship and CVC's. It's about managing an end-to-end process and translating ideas into impact by correctly designing, combining and aligning activities, and their interface. I present a framework and methodology that will provide a guide to corporate companies on the journey of building a Growth Machine beside the core business, in order to achieve new economic growth and create a more entrepreneurial culture.

As a change manager in large organizations, I had the nagging feeling that even after pursuing successful programs with concrete results, the organization would fall back into old habits as soon as I left the building. I realized that my interventions, aimed at enhancing the learning capabilities of individuals and teams, were incomplete, even though they did enable people to develop themselves further. I was forced to conclude that smart people who put the customer first and design systems that do things differently, can only create mediocre results. The answer lies in working on different fields simultaneously (processes, KPI's, governance, leadership), so that the organizational architecture changes.

What is a 10x Growth Machine?

The Growth Machine is a separate system (like an innovation lab, or independent business unit) that co-exists with the mothership and is managed by members of the executive board in the form of a venture board. The purpose of the Growth Machine is to ideate, validate and scale disruptive ventures. Incubation of ideas, collaboration with startups and potential acquisitions, are all part of this unit and follow the same innovations process, metrics, funding and protections by the venture board.

Why is this a big idea? Leaders often believe their organization is capable of doing anything. In reality, organizations fail because they force new innovations through their existing processes and profit formula, 'where to invest in and what are the margins?' Learning and experimentation stops, entrepreneurship and initiatives get killed. As a result, new entrants disrupt the incumbent and organizations vanish. Companies may succeed for many different reasons, but many of them fail for one: they *did not adapt* to the logic of the situation in which they found themselves. The logic of situations, from the interpersonal to larger economy, is always implicit, hidden and tacit and you have to figure it out without having the codebook in your hand.

As Steve Blank remarks: "A startup is not a smaller version of a big company. A startup is a temporary organization that is searching for a business model". The keyword here is *searching*. Lean startups validate their biggest business model risks by a hypothesis-driven way of *experimentation*. They build MVP's, a small/simple version of the product, to learn the most through a build-measure-learn rhythm. This way of working is very different from the regular operating model of a modern organization. A big company executes the existing business model and operates with the idea that it knows all the answers around the execution. They work according to the rhythm of writing plans and long budgeting cycles to avoid risks.

Aniruddha Kusurkar, global director consumer dairy at FrieslandCampina, formulates it as follows: "Big companies have a lot of processes for two main reasons. One reason is that to manage the risk, everything has one or two more zeros. Risk management is an aim in itself. We have a separation between thinking and doing. Senior people want control over what is happening from a risk perspective. Another reason is scattered resources, so you need to manage internal stakeholders for their resources. We have a whole system in place to protect the existing business".

The challenge is how to get corporations to behave more like the market and increase the rate of creative destruction to the level of the market itself, without losing control of present operations. Balancing learning, searching and destroying, while exploiting current business, may be very sensible advice, but it has proven difficult to implement. The data on corporate longevity as summarized in Chapter 1 is clear: companies that want to survive have to master the art of creative destruction; build for discontinuity and remake like the market. Joseph Schumpeter anticipated this transformation over half a century ago, when he observed: "The problem that is usually being visualized is how capitalism administers existing structures, whereas the relevant problem is how it creates and destroys them."

Most companies are pretty satisfied with their operating abilities, but (in general) dissatisfied with their ability to implement change. Why is this? The inherent conflict lies between the need for corporations to control existing operations and the need to create the kind of environment that will permit new ideas to flourish and old ones to die a timely death. This may require trading out traditional assets, challenging existing channels of distribution or making acquisitions. The challenge is that most corporations will find it impossible to outperform the market without abandoning their existing business model. Modern organizations are built on the assumption that they all need to exploit the current business, so let's have a deeper look at the differences between exploration and exploitation.

	Explore (discontinuity)	Exploit (continuity)
FUNCTION	• Searching for new business models. Figuring out how to destroy current business models	• Exploiting validated business models
MANAGEMENT	• Entrepreneurship	• Traditional management
PROCESS	• Iterative (build-measure-learn)	• Linear (waterfall method)
MEASUREMENT	• Innovation accounting	• Traditional accounting
STRUCTURE	• Loosely coupled network	• Process driven hierarchy
MINDSET	• 'I don't know'	• 'I have all the answers, and can perform'
TOOLS	• Business model canvas - customer development - Agile engineering	• Business plans
METRICS	• Amount paying customers • Returning paying customers • Costs per new customer	• Return on investment • Accountant rate return
VALUES	• Fast decision making • Customer obsession • Relentless learning • Intelligent failure = learning	• Sustain the status quo

Table 2.1 – The differences between exploration and exploitation

The list of variables is not complete, but it shows the differences in paradigms. While the exploitation paradigm is dominant in established companies, no organization started big. Every company started with entrepreneurs who were exploring, testing and searching for a business to scale, the *explore* paradigm. When companies start to grow, they find this entrepreneurial behavior annoying and chaotic and begin to eliminate it. The key is to recover this mentality and way of working, separate it from the core business and manage, as leaders, the balance and tensions between these two systems that are very different but have to live in symbiosis.

In the next paragraph, I describe the set of principles, processes and tools that are the foundation for developing such a system, the Growth Machine next to the mothership.

2.1   10x Growth Machine building blocks

The main question for companies is: "How can I execute my existing business and improve it, but at the same time create new growth models and leverage our resources for these two opposite things?"

The Growth Machine Framework (see Figure 1) is designed to build and develop a Growth Machine that can ideate, validate and scale corporate startups. This machine co-exists with the mothership and is loosely integrated with the different layers of management through a venture board governance setup. This approach will also facilitate more disruptive innovations and help with the digitalization of existing business models. It means that different processes are utilized to go from new idea to success, with different KPI's to measure success and a profit formula (which criteria do we use to allocate resources and prioritize?) that fits new growth business.

Training people in Lean Startup methodologies is not the only thing that needs to happen in order to achieve new growth. More building blocks need to be implemented to scale corporate startups successfully and develop an entrepreneurial culture.

These building blocks together form the foundation for my 10x Growth Machine Methodology.

The building blocks are:

Growth strategy	Growth governance	Corporate venture building	Growth culture	Scaling growth
Growth strategy and portfolio management	Lean innovation process and venture boards	Implementa-tion of growth strategies and a Lean startup way of working	Awareness and training in a new set of principles	How to scale the startup to a scaleup? Independent business unit? Spin out?
C-level align-ment	Venture boards			
	Growth policy playbook			
	Growth accounting			

Table 2.2 – 10x Growth Machine building blocks

1. Growth Strategy & Portfolio management
    • A portfolio of the innovation projects that are connected to the corporate strategy and its goals. This portfolio is developed around three playing fields: *Optimize the Core, Renew the Core* and *Future Growth*.

2. Growth governance
    • The Lean innovation process: a process to select, filter, fund and terminate corporate startups. The internal venture board governs the internal selection and funding process for corporate startups.
    • A growth policy playbook: create a set of new policies that facili-tates and stimulates innovation. Most impediments for innovation

are on the tactical level. For example: can we experiment with a new value proposition under an existing brand? Can we find a partner next month to create a thousand products instead of the regular 100,000?

- Growth Accounting: the essence is to define a metric system that measures progress of internal startups in a correct manner, and to connect their progress to the health of the innovation management process and the corporate strategy goals. Most startups don't make a lot of money, so the key is to show progress in a way that translates the learning of startups into a roadmap that leads to a healthy business case.

3.   Corporate venture building
- Small ninja teams working on the innovation portfolio projects in a Lean Startup way and build products and services that generate new income.

4.   Growth culture
- The culture in the Growth Machine is built on very different principles due to different processes, KPI's and ways of working. To execute in the Growth Machine, employees must eat, sleep and breathe these set of principles:
  - Think 10x bigger and bolder.
  - Customer obsession.
  - Scarcity mindset.
  - Relentless learning, relentless high standards.
  - Skeptic of proxies.
  - Adopting external trends.
  - Fast decision-making.
  - Ownership.

5.   Scaling growth
- This building block is about determining how to scale a corporate startup when it hits a recurring revenue model. Is it going to be a spin-out? Or are we setting up an independent business unit?

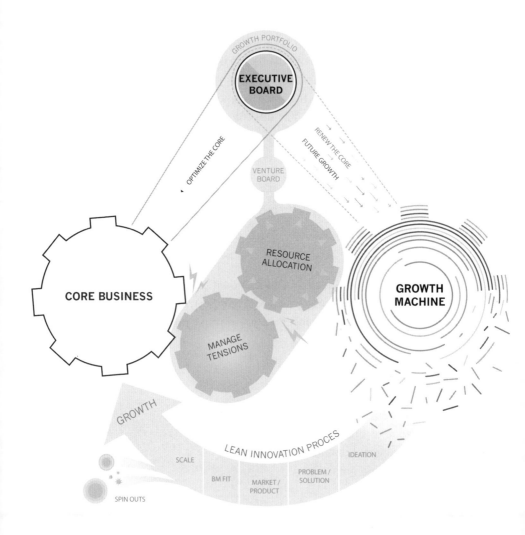

Figure 2.1 – The 10x Growth Machine

The 10x Growth Machine Methodology provides the building blocks and serves as the transformation path for established corporate organizations to serve three strategic goals:
1. Renewing the Core business – Redesign the core business for the future
2. Creating Future Growth engines – Create the new growth of the company
3. Scale the new – managing the startup to scale-up in the corporate

As Eric Ries says: "Entrepreneurship is always about institution-building, so it is necessarily about management." The 10x Growth Machine Methodology provides you with the principles and building blocks to navigate in a complex corporate environment, where the goal is to scale a more entrepreneurial way of management, one that enables you to build new growth engines, not by accident but by default.

FrieslandCampina, a global dairy company

By Lianne Dingemanse – Manager corporate accelerators

Why did FrieslandCampina start their version of the 10x Growth Machine, the Milkubator program?

The world is changing rapidly and disruptive innovations are being brought to the market at a faster pace than ever before. To win in the market, FrieslandCampina needs to become faster and consumer and customer-centric, while being agile.

We decided to start the Milkubators (our corporate accelerators). The goal of the Milkubators is to find our second or third Horizon disruptive innovations, which will create our future business. By keeping the Milkubators separate from the corporate, we are enabling the teams to completely focus on using the Lean Startup methodology. The goal is to find new 100-million businesses, we also want to create a change in mindset and behavior in the rest of the organization. The Milkubator program also has a building pillar capability through which we provide training, masterclasses and on the job support. By providing these new tools and skill sets, we hope to enable change, which will further create focus, speed and a consumer/customer-centric approach.

How well has this program, until now, been adopted by the company? What is going well? What needs improvement?

We started the Milkubator program with four teams – teams that were willing to try something different and new. Now, a year and a half later, the program has grown globally and more business units are adopting the Lean Startup way in various formats. We have also applied the build, measure, learn principle to the implementation of the program itself, and slowly we are seeing the results of the Lean Startup and agile ways of working. The company is becoming more consumer- and customer-centric, identifies and validates a couple of potential new growth models and is gaining a lot by also killing ideas, which generally would have continued, resulting in higher costs. Though we are at the start of the journey, FrieslandCampina sees this as a long-term investment and the next important step is to align the way of working across functions.

Can you describe the governance model around Milkubator?

The business supports Milkubators. The sponsor should always be a business sponsor, who can coach the team, remove hurdles, leverage its network to help the team and have bi-weekly sprint demos with the team. The investor is the Business Group President (depending on the business group to which the topic belongs). The CEO supports the idea and is updated on the progress. The Milkubators receive resources (time, money, people) for a fixed period, usually three to five months. After that, we have an investor meeting at which they present a progress report, based on the stages they have reached. Within FrieslandCampina we have four phases: customer discovery, customer validation, business model validation and growth. These investor meetings are a Go/No-go moment in which the sponsor and president decide if they want to continue with this new venture. The Milkubators do not have to work with our 'standard' project management stage gate process, only when capex is involved. The reason why we treat Milkubators differently is to create short decision lines, which allows way more speed and agility.

What did you learn about Lean Startup methodology in the context of Milkubator?

Within the Milkubators, we use the Lean Startup methodology as a tool to create structure, focus and speed. This methodology helps us to focus more on our consumers and customers, and always to test our assumptions. Through our capability pillar, we also want to embed (parts of) the Lean Startup methodology in our normal product innovation projects. In certain categories we see a decline in growth and, with this way of working, we can quickly identify where the problem in the current business model lies and prototype cheap and fast solutions to fix it.

If we look at the FrieslandCampina organization, was it equipped to facilitate rapid prototyping and embrace the concept of a minimal viable product?

The processes and procedures within FrieslandCampina are super-efficient and, like any other large FMCG, entirely structured to produce large volumes efficient at the lowest possible cost. We have an excellent R&D Centre in which the Milkubator teams can test, learn and improve the prototypes in our kitchen or lab. However, as soon as they want to move to small commercially viable production batches, it becomes a challenge. Our factories are not equipped for that. That is one reason why, for some teams, we chose to first work with external manufacturers, and as soon as production grows, perhaps take it back into one of our factories. That said, some products are also produced somewhere else, because they are so new, we do not have the production facilities ourselves. We then identify, with the help of our innovation partner Innoleaps, which partners we need to embed in our innovation ecosystem.

How do you scale a successful project? Which criteria do you use?

We expect that a few ventures will enter this phase within the year and examples of the criteria we use for this are:
- Is the business model validated and can it work on larger scale?
- Can we scale this business to multiple countries/areas?
- Has this business the potential to provide substantial EBIT contribution?

When the Milkubator reaches the phase to scale, we will return the business to the business unit in which the Milkubator team can leverage the existing route-to-market and sales engine of the unit or country. In the cases when a venture is substantially different from any other business and has potential for growth, we will decide to make it a separate business unit. The speed with which we have identified and validated new growth models is remarkable and way higher than we could have achieved in our core business organizational architecture.

What are the next steps for the program? Improvements? Bigger ambitions?

In 2019 our ambition is to continue with the Milkubator teams and focus on making these a success. Some of the current teams will stop or be embedded back in the normal business, creating room to start new teams, who will search for disruptive innovations.

Next to this, we also started Micro battles. These use the same way of working (build, measure, learn) and have entirely dedicated, cross-functional teams working in an agile/Scrum way. The difference is that these teams focus on accelerating the growth of existing business or innovations closer to the core. We believe that bringing this way of working to our core will create speed, more consumer focus and in the end, faster results.

What would you recommend to a reader who wants to start a program like this?

Do it! We started two years ago with this program, and it brought us many benefits. However, the most significant advantage will be the cultural change in mindset and behavior: putting customers and consumers first, always testing your assumptions, focusing on fewer, but potentially more significant initiatives and the fact that stopping an initiative is also OK.

2.2   10x Growth Machine principles
   – in pursuit of excellence

"What doesn't make you the best at what you do, makes you ordinary. What makes you ordinary can never make you the best. You can't beat that logic. People have been trying to do that for years." – Lee Thayer

Building a *Growth Machine* in a corporate environment is challenging. Besides setting up a governance structure that enables fast learning and entrepreneurship, the way of working is very different to the way people think and act in the mothership. Where a big company is setup to execute and has values like risk avoidance, stability and control, people in the *Growth Machine* need to have an entrepreneurial mindset to do the opposite. To build a new business requires top performance, and conventional thinking will get us nowhere. Personal leadership is the key to break the conventional mindset in something unconventional. People who challenge themselves and push their own boundaries have the ability to make it through. This means that people should be selected according to the criteria quite different to that, which applies in the big company. We don't look for the experienced VP sales from a big company. Why? We need searchers, entrepreneurs, not people who can close the deal based on the script, all of the corporate startups have no script for sales. Their goal is to construct a repeatable sales map, based on validated learning from the market that shows how the business can grow. Let's have a look at the most important principles on which the Growth Machine builds the operation and execution.

Think 10x bigger and bolder

Intrapreneurs should push themselves to think bold when it comes to how they want to commercialize their idea. Come up with ten options on potential revenue streams. 50 million in revenues? How can we create a business model that can bring in 500 million? This mentality forces the team to think big and avoid mental traps and habits from the past.

Customer obsession
Within Amazon, this is a key principle. They started creating new ideas or developing new products with the end-consumer in mind. From that perspective they work backwards. According to Jeff Bezos, customer obsession is the best antidote for corporate politics and bureaucracy. Every decision should be made with the end-consumer in mind.

Scarcity mindset
We teach our clients to work with the resources available. *Bricolage* is a French word that stands for creating solutions with the means available. Evidently, when teams have too much money or time, creativity is killed. People get lazy. We bootstrap teams and challenge them to setup experiments with the biggest learning impact, using the smallest amount of resources possible. This is where creativity is born; it thrives with a disciplined way of working.

How good you are at what you do, is revealed solely by how well you per-form *under adversity*. Make the logic of adversity your ally.

Relentless learning, relentless high standards

You can't beat that logic. People have been trying to do that for years. I will hire somebody with bigger learning capabilities and curiosity over somebody with experience. Experience can cause a person to be biased and is not willing to change his or her approach. The first person will beat the second one, relentlessly. First of all, the learners figure out how to fix the challenge presented instead of being biased. Secondly, because most of the time they have very high-quality standards for themselves and they always over-perform. Learners are continually raising the bar and driving their teams to deliver high-quality products, services, and processes. Leaders ensure that defects do not get sent down the line and the prob-lems that are fixed stay fixed.

Sceptic of proxies

Popular psychology ideologies are basically about the process: get the process right and everything will turn out right. If it was that simple, we would all be very successful doing what everybody else is doing. That is exactly what we are doing and nobody can be equally successful. An instrument is as good as the person who plays it and the more compe-tent a person is, the better the output of the process. The more trained you are as a violinist, the better you can master the instrument and can improvise on the spot. This takes hours, days, weeks, months and years of practice.

Accountability

Words are not accomplishments. It is typically what people offer instead of an accomplishment. The more accomplished people in an organization are, the less they talk about it. Consider these thoughts:

- The less people achieve, the more they feel the need to talk about it.
- Communication fills the void left by having no clear purpose, or by fail-ing to accomplish what needed to be accomplished.
- Most communication in organizations is in lieu of accomplishment. Or

it may simply be as irrelevant as the people who engage in it, as a substitute for purposeful performance.

Accountability means owning the outcome – not the talk. To develop a Growth Machine, accountability is the tool that you, as the leader, must wield. You, as well as people in your organization, must be:

- Accountable for statements made.
- Accountable for the promises that were made to anyone inside or outside the organization.
- Accountable for an implicit promise.
- Accountable for every accomplishment you and they claim, explicitly or implicitly, and for the ramifications of whatever occurs as a result of your or their failure to perform.
- Accountable for developing all of the competencies required to accomplish what you have signed on to accomplish.

There is no accountability where there are no consequences for failing to accomplish that which was agreed on.

Adopting external trends
Customer obsession is about understanding the outside world. What kind of developments do we see at the periphery of the market which help us to delight our customers? What kind of business models arise from which we can learn? At the core of an innovative high-performing organization are business models experimenting with new technologies. Survival of the fittest is not about the strongest or the biggest, but about how fast you can adapt to your environment.

Fast decision-making
Consensus-driven decision-making is the enemy of new endeavors. Consensus is driven by politics, positions and other irrelevant themes when it comes to building new growth models. Jeff Bezos uses the 'disagree but commit' motto. It actually means you can disagree, but still need to commit. It also means that in our work we make decisions based on 50% or 60% of the available information. We move forward with 'good enough' information.

Disciplined communication

In general, communication is viewed as sending information from person A to B. This is a linear and very limited view of the process, as all mistakes are made in – and results achieved through – communication. Communication is a process of subjective interpretation by the receiver of the message. So, what you want to achieve as a sender, can only be achieved if the receiver agrees, which is exactly why communication should be disciplined. The more disciplined the communication is in your company, the more successful it becomes, leading to clear roles and accountability. Clear meeting structure, an understanding of why people join meetings, what is expected from them and what the goals are. High-performance starts on a small and practical level.

2.3   10x Growth Machine Canvas

Like the Business Model Canvas, the 10x Growth Machine Canvas is a visual tool that executives can use to build their roadmap of implementation. It is the *how to* tool, to translate the 10x Growth Machine Framework, in an actionable roadmap for C-level (to align on and implement). It helps the board starting the innovation journey. It perfectly relates to the market navigator toolset[12], which helps to decide where to play and how to win. When this is clear, the business and value proposition canvas [13] helps you to understand all the relevant elements in the new venture.

In order to understand *the situation as it is,* I developed an *innovation capability assessment* which helps with developing the roadmap, respecting the unique position of the client's company.

Growth Machine Canvas

INNOVATION STRATEGY   **INNOVATION GOVENANCE**

Venture board	Growth Transformation Communication
Innovation portfolio	
Innovation proces & metered funding	Innovation accounting metrics

(Circle contents, top to bottom: Innovation Thesis / Strategic opportunity areas / Growth gap analysis)

Figure 2.2 – The 10x Growth Machine Canvas

Trigger questions to get started with the 10x Growth Machine Canvas

Innovation strategy

1. Innovation thesis
   - What does innovation mean for us? Which definition/boundaries of innovation do we have?
   - Do we allocate resources in all three playing fields? If not, why?
   - What terminology do we use to describe innovation?
   - What do you see happening in your category/market (other large players, digital giants, startups, etc.) that is changing the nature of the game and the ability to win consumers in the coming years, and grow profitably?
   - Based on that, can you summarize your point of view on the opportunities and challenges for the company to accelerate innovation?

2. Growth opportunity areas
   - Where is the money to be made in the future? Which domains do we want to focus on in order to develop new growth models? See the Tool Guide to determine your Growth Opportunity Areas.
   - Do we see changes for us in the value chain?
   - Can we identify underserved or unsolved consumer problems?
   - What capabilities and assets do we have and does this give us an unfair advantage?

3. Growth gap analysis
   - If we project our current earnings in our current business over the next five years, what would be our growth gap?
   - Which external factors can influence this gap (positive or negative)?

Innovation governance

1. Growth transformation communication
    - Did we communicate to the organization our view of the future of our company? Which growth opportunities do we see?
    - Did we communicate to the company how we want to pursue these new growth opportunities?
    - Are staff departments (IT, Legal, HR) trained in Lean Startup methodologies, so that they are aware of the fact that innovation teams work in a very different way (hypothesis-driven, fast experimentation) to pursue a very different goal (search for a repeatable business model) in comparison to the existing operating model of the core business?

2. Venture board
    - Did we install, in the relevant categories/business units, a venture board that is the gatekeeper of future funding?
    - Is the venture board aware and do they embrace Growth Accounting metrics as a way to measure progress?
    - Does the venture board play the role of central clearing house of information over the innovation portfolio for the organization?

3. Innovation portfolio
    - Is there alignment on the innovation portfolio over the three playing fields on senior level management?
    - Does the innovation portfolio play a central role in growth board meetings?
    - Are metrics for success defined for different layers of the portfolio?
        - Strategic level: When is our Growth Machine successful?
        - Innovation process: Do we have enough qualitative concepts to pursue the three playing fields? Does our process function properly? How many teams churn? How many teams move forward in the process? To what cost?
        - Operational level: does every team and concept have specific metrics for success in place and are the business sponsors aware of these metrics?

4. Innovation process and metered funding
    - Is there an end-to-end Lean innovation process, with phases and clear milestones that need to be reached in order to get future funding?
    - Is this end-to-end innovation process embedded in 'the way of working' when it comes to innovation in categories/business units?
    - Is there awareness and alignment among growth board members, that funding is automatically secured when corporate startups reach these milestones?
    - Does Finance understand the principles of metered funding and innovation accounting metrics?

5. Growth Accounting metrics
    - Are board members, GMs and directors, trained in Growth Accounting?
    - Is Finance trained in Growth Accounting?
    - Are the corporate startup team members trained in Growth Accounting and coached in metrics for success and the 'one metric that matters[14]' in their business model?

6. Growth transformation communication
    - How would you describe the level of awareness and commitment of the business leaders on innovation? Who are the most supportive, and who are the most resistant?
    - What is the overarching rationale that the board needs to communicate internally when it comes to innovation?

 *Also have a look at the **innovation capability assessment** tool for a better understanding of possible blind spots or topics to work on when it comes to your Growth Machine.*

In the following chapters the building blocks in the 10x Growth Machine Methodology are discussed, starting with growth strategy and portfolio management.

Points to ponder

There is hope for established companies to innovate systematically on new horizons. Besides training people in Lean Startup or other customer-driven methodologies, the 10x Growth Machine Methodology provides the other crucial building blocks that need to be implemented. To make this happen follow a couple of steps:

1. First determine with the board or as the board how you are scoring on these building blocks. You can use the 'innovation capability assessment' to spark discussions around the most crucial topics. Use the 10x Growth Machine Canvas and its checklist to determine which building blocks and activities need attention in your company.
2. For innovation to be taken seriously, use the concept of the 'growth gap' to set a clear revenue objective that innovation should hit in a three to four-year timespan.
3. This makes it possible to setup a roadmap for different activities, internal incubation, corporate startup collaboration and acquisitions on new horizons that should lead to bridge the growth gap.
4. Determine 'growth opportunity areas' with senior leadership to align as a group about where the company should invest its money in. To determine these growth opportunity areas and ignite the right discussions, you can use the checklist Guide to determine Growth Opportunity Area's.

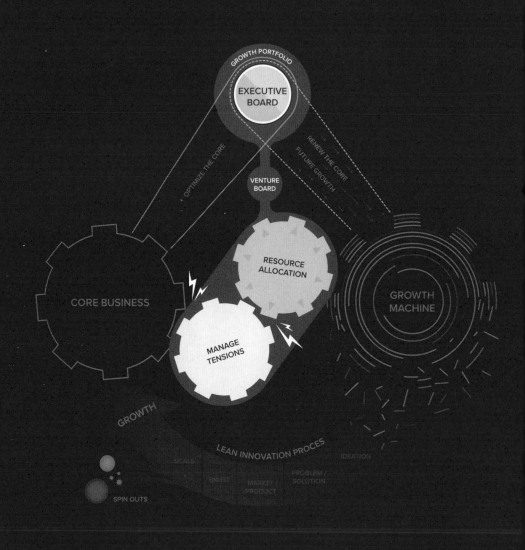

Chapter 3
Growth Strategy and Portfolio management

In this chapter we discuss the building block 'innovation portfolio', how growth strategy should inform a portfolio of innovation initiatives and explain the concept of the 'three playing fields' (Optimize the Core, Renew the Core and Future Growth) further. A crucial element for success is to understand where to focus energy and resources, when it comes to growth and to understand how the companies' portfolio is performing.

Different types of growth strategies will be discussed, in particular the disruptive strategy, from which new growth is derived. We look at the various growth strategies15 that can be deployed in certain market situations and explain how identifying customer needs (based on the job to be done) plays a crucial role. We finish with how the portfolio management process works and emphasize the part of the resource allocation process.

3.1   Disruption and understanding the periphery

"The periphery provides an external market benchmark for the pace of change in the economy" – Richard Foster and Sarah Kaplan

The focus on innovation for big companies is making a better product. Every company needs to make certain gross margins, and if you need to make 40% gross margins, the company will probably kill projects that cannot deliver on these margins. According to Clayton Christensen[16], the values of big successful companies evolve in two predictable dimensions. First, concerning sustaining innovation, creating better and better products will lead to additional overhead costs, which in turn, makes gross margins that looked attractive seem unattractive at a later point. Company's values change as they migrate up-market. The second question, relating to a change in values, is how big a business should be to be interesting. Because the company's stock price is represented by the discounted present value of its projected earnings stream, most managers feel compelled to maintain a constant growth rate.

For a 10-million-euro company it takes a 2.5-million-euro new business opportunity to have a 25% growth. For a 10-billion-euro company a 2.5-billion-euro growth opportunity. Opportunities that excite small companies are not large enough to be interesting for big companies. As a result, the bittersweet reward of success is that as companies become larger, they lose the ability to enter the small emerging markets where the money is to be made in the future. Small opportunities of today can be the growth models of tomorrow.

Understanding the companies forming at the periphery is necessary to gain strategic insights into the future possibilities of the industry, but it is also essential for revealing the most pressing unmet customer needs. These companies are trying out or exploring the idea of selling products to some currently dissatisfied customer group.

To understand where small opportunities arise, it is essential to identify early warning signals. Today's opportunities can become tomorrow's threats when neglected. Early warning signals are, for example:

1. The entrance of new business models in the market.
2. VC investments in a particular domain.
3. Regulatory changes.

 For a full checklist of 'early warning signals' check the 'disruptive analysis checklist'. All tools are available at www.10xgrowthmachine.com

If we connect the 'early warning signals' with portfolio thinking, we can determine in which markets disruption is a possibility that connects with our portfolio. Which projects deal with this particular market opportunity? Which startups do we need to collaborate with? And if parts of the existing business are under threat, which projects are aimed at repositioning (digitalization) the core business? So how do you determine the disruption threat of your current company?

Christensen proposes a systematic way to chart the path and pace of disruption so that you can fashion a complete strategic response. To determine whether a missile will hit you dead-on or will be a near miss, you need to:

- Identify the strengths of your disrupter's business model.
- Identify your relative advantages.
- Evaluate the conditions that would help or hinder the disrupter from co-opting your current advantages in the future.

Disrupters are created in incubation and accelerator programs. Startup-bootcamp is such a player, functioning on the periphery of the market – a place where a couple of disruptors were born and found their way to scale.

Interview with Patrick de Zeeuw, co-founder of Startupbootcamp, Innoleaps and The Talent institute, about corporate startup collaboration.

Why should corporates collaborate with startups or scale-ups? What is their aim/benefit?

Corporate startup collaboration, CSC as we call it, is becoming a part of modern innovation management. The benefits from a successful CSC can be enormous and have a big impact on global corporations as well as the scale-ups.

Let me give you an example. A few years ago, Munich RE started collaborating with one of the scale-ups from our Startupbootcamp portfolio to solve a specific problem. Eventually, that successful collaboration let to a strategic investment from Munich RE into Relayr. From that moment, Munich RE, as a shareholder and board member of the company, had a better view on the impact of Relayr, both in the near future and on Munich RE's core business. Last year Munich RE decided that Relayr's technology and business model could become disruptive for its own business and could also create significant new growth opportunities for Munich RE. They decided to acquire Relayr for 300 million dollars, 4 or 5 years after the company started. This all began with a small collaboration, proving that both sides could work together and add value to each other. The Relayr story is great because it shows how strategically important startup collaboration can be, both for corporates and startups.

How can the collaborations between big and small companies become successful?

It's difficult to innovate in a fast and effective way within a large global organization. I firmly believe it's possible, but you need to have entrepreneurs or intrapreneurs with the right mind and skill set, incentivized in a way, other than through a straightforward salary. These people can deal with the blood, sweat and tears it takes to innovate and develop new products when there can be a big up-sell at the end of the tunnel.

Can intrapreneurship become a career path in a large, established company?

Startups that never collaborated with corporates are not realistic in their estimation of the time it can take to get a contract with a corporate. Corporates should manage these expectations upfront. A startup's biggest asset is time, but when it takes eight months to close a deal, the startup might be dead. The question to ask before starting a collaboration is: "Are we both equipped in the right way to start collaborating?" Startups are in search of new business models and solving pains in the market, but a large organization needs to be aware that early-stage startups have not always figured out the solution. This might change over time. The startups should be critical of the request from a corporate to develop customized solutions. Before you know it, the startup is not building their scalable product anymore but is merely an agency for solving the problems of the corporate. From that perspective, for corporates, it is more advantageous to collaborate with a scale-up because they have a product, they solve a problem and can deliver.

Learning is a crucial part of being an innovative company. How would you advise the executives of big corporations on this topic?

Most people working in big companies have a learning and knowledge gap. Students from MBA's or universities learned to master a toolbox that applied to large companies. It was about how to grow and manage a global company. However, the business environment has become very challenging, a place where customer behavior changes, new companies enter the market with new business models and new technology accelerates these changes more than ever before. So how to leverage the changes in the market and customer needs? To see these changes as opportunities instead of threats, it takes the mindset shift all corporations need to make. The question then becomes, "How to behave, how to think and how to operate as a startup in a large organization?" We see more executives willing to understand, embrace and implement this way of working.

Let's dive into the mechanics of disruption. To *disrupt*, in entrepreneurial parlance, now in general means "innovate in a new or surprising way." But in the *Harvard Business Review*, Clayton Christensen himself added clarity to the term, along with co-authors Michael E. Raynor and Rory MacDonald. "Too many people," they write, "use the term loosely to invoke the concept of innovation in support of whatever it is they wish to do."

To clarify disruption: "What happens when the incumbents are so focused on pleasing their most profitable customers that they neglect or misjudge the needs of their other segments?" This gives startups a way of entering the market at the low-end and starting to climb up the market to serve the high-end customer segments.

From that perspective, Uber is not disrupting the taxi business for two reasons. First of all, according to Christensen's theory, disruptive innovations originate in low-end or new-market footholds, and he (and his co-authors) assert that Uber did not originate in either. It is difficult to claim that the company found a low-end opportunity, as it would have meant that taxi service providers had overshot the needs of several customers by making cabs too plentiful, too easy to use and too clean. Neither did Uber primarily target non-consumers, the people who found the existing alternatives so expensive or inconvenient that they took public transport or drove themselves instead. Uber was launched in San Francisco (a well-served taxi market) and Uber's customers were generally people already in the habit of hiring rides. Nor does it signal, from Christensen and his co-authors, disrespect for Uber's impact. "Uber has quite arguably been increasing total demand – that's what happens when you develop a better, less-expensive solution to a widespread customer need," they write. As we'll discuss later on, offering a better and cheaper service than the existing alternatives is always a good strategy.

"Disrupters, on the other hand, start by appealing to low-end or over-looked consumers and then migrate into the mainstream market," they continue. "Uber has gone in exactly the opposite direction, by building a position in the mainstream market first and subsequently appealing to historically overlooked segments." This can only be achieved with aggressive investments from their side. We know the huge investment numbers that are associated with the growth of Uber.

Characteristics of low-end disruption:

1. Does not give you something that is better, but rather 'Good enough' quality.
2. The customers that they target are at the bottom of the market, not the top. These customers are over-served by other products.
3. The root ability to deliver it for low-cost.

Leaders of the industry in essence will flee and not fight with entrants that provide low-end disruption. This is because their rationale would be, 'Why would we spend time, money and energy fighting against small companies in markets where we earn less?'

Low-end disruption in the automobile sector

Though I was a little boy, I still remember my father saying, "The Toyota Corona is the ugliest car in the world." Boy! I was impressed, that must be some ugly car! Toyota did not enter the US market with the Lexus, instead they came with this small, 'ugly' and cheap little car, named Corona. It served a customer group at the low-end of the market, while General Motors and Ford made big cars for the high-end consumers. They paid no attention to this funky little car with its low margins. GM sent down the Pinto to the low end of the market, but it just made no sense if you can make bigger cars for people with bigger wallets. Surely, the Corona became the Corolla, Tercel, 4Runner and then the Lexus. So as you see, the Corona was an entryway to move upmarket with new models like the Lexus.

Being disruptive is something different for every company. Dell Computer, for instance, began by selling computers over the telephone and, for Dell, the initiative to start selling over the internet was a sustainable innovation. It helped Dell make more money within its already existing structure. So it was not surprising when Dell successfully adopted internet retailing. Their model, from this perspective, was not disruptive. For Compaq, Hewlett-Packard and IBM, marketing directly to customers was disruptive, because of its impact on their retail channel partners. They couldn't make room for internet distribution within their existing organizations, and so their attempts to incorporate this new channel were far less successful.

Another type of disruption that Christensen identified is a 'new market' disruption. The interesting element about creating a new market is that you automatically need to target non-consumption. In other words, there is a population segment out there that previously did not have the ability to reach or access the product. Products or services, as a 'new market' disruption, performed less well in *traditional* attributes, but improved performance in new attributes – typically by simplicity and convenience. They redefined performance in ways that appealed to the non-consumers.

New market disruption characteristics[17]:

1. It targets non-consumption.
2. The providers are able to make money at much lower prices per unit sold.
3. Product provides lower performance in *traditional* attributes, but improved performance in new attributes – typically simplicity and convenience.

New market and low-end disruption in the Smartphone industry

As industry observers are keenly aware, Android and iOS dominate the smart-phone landscape in terms of shipments as well as developer mindshare. This duopoly is a result of two major disruptions that the mobile industry saw in rapid succession. The first was a "new market disruption", caused by the iPhone, which introduced the paradigm of mobile computing. The second was a low-end disruption, caused by the Android operating system, which reduced barriers of entry to the smartphone market and caused deep commoditization.

A new market disruption changes the basis of competition in the marketplace and initially competes against non-consumption. In the mobile industry, the iPhone brought the concept of mobile computing to the mainstream market and initially did not have much of an impact on incumbents. Over time, performance improvement enabled a wider range of tasks to be performed on the iPhone, which pulled in customers from competing legacy mobile platforms (such as Blackberry, Windows Mobile, etc.) and personal computing platforms as well.

In contrast to this dynamic, a low-end disruption takes root in low-end segments of an existing market, which may be over-served. Improved technology enables new business models to emerge that are based on lower cost structures. Low-end disrupters with extendable business models then move up-market by offering good enough products at lower price points. The Android operating system was a classic low-end disruption, as it introduced a modular platform and ecosystem that allowed less experienced handset makers to build compelling products without major investment in software.

New-market disruption refers to businesses that compete against non-consumption in lower-margin sectors of a market. Similar to low-end disruption, the products offered are generally seen as *good enough*, and the emerging business is able to be profitable at these lower prices. The main difference between the two types of disruption lies in the fact that low-end disruption focuses on over-served customers, and new-market disruption focuses on underserved customers.

HBX new market disruption

Who does not know Harvard? The prestigious university for the lucky few. Well not anymore. Harvard delivers probably the best MBA students in the world for a high-class price. As we know, organizations focus in general on their best-paying customers in the highest tiers. But universities noticed that developments like online learning and in-company MBA programs were becoming attractive alternatives for doing a very expensive program at Harvard. So they used the online learning technology to build HBX – an online learning platform and community that delivers online learning for people all over the world for lower prices. Suddenly, many more people all over the world got access to Harvard and could share in the knowledge available to this institute. Thus Harvard creates a new market by combining online learning technology with the assets they already possess: their prestigious brand and the world class content.

Merging, buying and competing against yourself are the three options you have when disruptive innovations emerge. How can you tell if disruption is afoot? The customers you need to notice, are the ones that have already left you, or those at the bottom of the market. These people don't need or want the products you offer. Find them and figure out why they left. They can point you to disruptive innovation, right when it is emerging.

 See the checklist: The disruptive strategy checklist for venture board investors

3.2   Growth Portfolio management
– The link between strategy and execution

There are some known methods, such as scenario planning, that can be used to create different future states based on critical uncertainties for the company. Long-term trends are analyzed and prioritized; versions of possible futures are developed. However, the company remains open to a wide range of alternative futures, many of which are unrealistic. So how do we create a strategy that is resilient in all futures?

Unfortunately, what we mostly end up with is a highly abstract vision statement. The problem is that companies try to see the future from their present viewpoint and assume that their current products and services will be relevant in the future. Most of the time, this will lead to an assessment of the future, not more than two or three years down the line, with comforting results: our products will still earn money. In addition, the annual planning process is often performed as a budgeting exercise, which inevitably makes the plans that emerge focus largely on improving the core business margins. Resources are allocated within the existing structures of the business and the organization is caught in the present.

All of the above traps in strategic planning, can lead to a failure of a long-term strategy, which in turn, leads to a bigger problem – a fundamental disconnection between strategy and innovation. While strategy without innovation leads to incrementalism, innovation without strategy leads to a real shortage of executive commitment. The first you can recognize in companies that only have competencies in sustaining innovation/Optimize the Core. The second you can detect when innovation labs need to hustle for resources and money, and they are not busy with the fundamental challenges the company is facing. New growth initiatives can get killed by top-management before they are given the chance to live.

 See the checklist: Innovation director, Is your board onboard?

We should ask ourselves questions like: "How will customer behavior change in 2030 when we look at changing technological developments, regulatory changes, etc.? What are the *jobs to be done* for customer groups in our markets? What are the insecurities in our environment, which we cannot affect and that have a huge impact on our business? How can we craft a strategy that will hold up in all scenarios?" Corporate strategy should take root in a balanced innovation portfolio, where we determine experiments in known, but also unknown, markets. Whatever we learn from the experiments should loop back into the corporate strategy process.

While strategy without innovation leads to incrementalism, innovation without strategy leads to a real shortage of executive commitment.

 No ideas on where to grow? Use the tool: Guide to determine 'Growth Opportunity Area's

CEO, worried about the quality of your strategy process? See the checklist: Evaluate the quality of your companies' strategic planning, at www.10xgrowthmachine.com

Venture capitalists use an investment thesis that focuses on the investment strategy. They identify future domains of interest and start building a portfolio of startups in the domains they invest in. Union Square Ventures, for example, only invests in mobile web-services. An innovation thesis points out what the innovation objectives are, how it relates to the corporate strategy and is clear on what the company would invest in and what not. To do this in a proper way, I provide a couple of tools and models that can be used.

With the portfolio tool, we connect the three playing fields for innovation (Optimize the Core, Renew the Core and Future Growth) with an innovation process (per phase explained in Chapter 4) to see the progress that projects are making in the innovation process. In the tool Corporate startup maturity – metered funding, I have written down the milestones per phase in the innovation process that the venture teams should hit before moving further.

In order to achieve 10x growth, a company should work simultaneously on the three playing fields and think about three options: build, partner or acquire. Do we build the innovation ourselves? Who can we partner with to make it happen? Or can we acquire a company that performs well on a certain capability the company does not have? Or should we acquire a company that already solves the identified pain point from the consumer in the market?

The 10x Growth Machine Portfolio

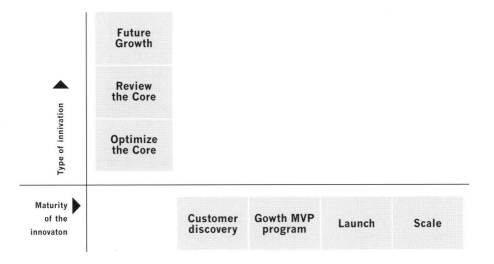

Figure 3.1 – The 10x Growth portfolio

In order to demonstrate the different types of innovation that companies can manage, I created the 10x Growth Machine portfolio framework. While the three Horizons of McKinsey focus on a specific timeframe, in which Horizon 3 takes the most time to develop growth, I deliberately let the timeframe go. Why? There is a prevailing myth in some boardrooms that investing in Horizon 3 is not interesting due to the length of time it takes to reach a certain maturity level. Nowadays, cash is available in abundance and technology enables fast growth. These two elements combined make it an obvious necessity to invest today in Future Growth innovation.

Optimize the Core represents those core businesses most readily identified with the company's name and those that provide the greatest profits and cash flow. Here the focus is on improving performance to maximize the remaining value. Think of a product innovation or the hundreds of little improvements that your company implements every day or every week to stay ahead of the curve. These innovations are the most achievable and are critical in order to keep your customer base happy and maintain your competitive edge in the current market. To stay relevant in your market over the years, it is necessary to place bigger bets, which redefine your business and/or open up completely new opportunities.

Renew the Core encompasses emerging opportunities, including new entrepreneurial ventures, which are likely to generate substantial profits in the future, but could require considerable investment. Such examples are the Apple Watch, Amazon's Kindle or the introduction of the newsfeed of Facebook. Although these innovations can relate to your existing product and business focus (i.e. digital books vs physical books), Renew the Core innovations are bigger ideas that take place outside your existing products' budget and activities. For product-oriented companies, think about creating digital services around the core products.

The playing field Future Growth contains ideas for profitable growth down the road, for instance small ventures such as research projects, pilot programs or minority stakes in new businesses. These small ventures can define a new market category and are often described as breakthrough innovations. They represent ideas that aren't extensions of your existing products or services. Google Glass is such an example (though it failed).

Something that might work and has the potential to become a break-through innovation is the driverless car. Future Growth innovations are Amazon's Web Services (AWS) and the iPad, having created a completely new category. In the Growth Machine model this is represented by create Future Growth.

Future Growth innovations require a vision, along with the stubbornness to achieve that vision in the face of all challenges and short-term priorities. Jeff Bezos admitted that it took them three tries to get their third-party seller business to work. Today, there are more than 2 million third-party vendors on Amazon, accounting for about 40% of all items sold. Jeff Bezos summed up the opportunity perfectly in an interview with *Wired*, back in 2011: "If everything you do needs to work on a three-year time horizon, then you're competing against a lot of people. But if you're willing to invest in a seven-year time horizon, you're now competing against a fraction of those people, because very few companies are willing to do that."

Netflix

Netflix is a good example of following a strategy that deliberately invests resources in different playing fields. By repositioning their core proposition, from offline DVD rental to an online streaming service, it started the 'disruptive trajectory' for Blockbuster and other DVD rental chains and all other small, local video stores. Besides that, Netflix protected its core business from being disrupted, which is the first transformation: Renewing the Core business. The aim here is to protect the daily business and to provide a steady cash flow to finance the second transformation, i.e. creating new growth engines. In comparison to other players, Netflix became disruptive with their own content production and their offer to access all of the content through a direct-to-consumer subscription model.

Portfolio management is a fundamental innovation capability used to dynamically plan, align, and optimize innovation investments. It serves as the link between innovation strategy and project execution, providing business leaders with the insight, data and visibility to improve decision-making for funding the right mix of projects across all playing fields. When performing well, portfolio management discipline:
- Ensures alignment between strategy and funded projects in the innovation pipeline.
- Optimizes resource loading for priority projects.
- Establishes clear project priorities.
- Ensures appropriate balance of projects by innovation type and risk profile.

In most companies, portfolio review is the same as the annual budget meetings. Though markets change fast, from the perspective of top priority projects and the resource allocation process, portfolio reviews should be a dynamic process in which new insights, like strategic pivots and project variances, are taken into account by the senior team that is overlooking the portfolio.

	Optimize the core	Renew the core	Future Growth
GOAL	Efficiency BM optimization	Revitalizing existing categories/products BM innovation	New growth BM Transformation
TECH	Using Tech to become faster, cheaper, better	Using tech to innovate the BM Model SMAQ	Using tech to change the essence of the company SMAQ+DARQ
COMPLEXITY OF CHANGE INTERNAL	First order change; Improving existing rules and policies. Solving problems and fixing mistakes	Second order change; Change on the level of rules and the rationale behind the change. Learning to learn	Third order change; Change on the value of rules and the rationale behind the change and the principles of the company
COMPLEXITY OF CHANGE EXTERNAL	Minimum ?	Medium ??	Complex ???
MARKET	Existing Market/ or internal	Existing Markets + resegmenting existing markets	New markets/ new products
SPACE	Internal execution	Separate first from the core business later integrate	Separate from the core business

Table 3.1 – Three types of innovation

In the table 3.1 I have summarized important characteristic of each innovation. Digital transformation is often used, but rarely well-defined. When we look at Renew the Core innovations, can tech be used to innovate certain elements in the existing business model? Can we innovate around our channels? Should we build an e-commerce channel to sell directly to consumers? Can we use data analytics to personalize our existing offerings for specific customers? In order to do this, you need to have a basic infrastructure in place around *Social media*, *Mobile*, *Analytics* and *Cloud* (SMAC). Chris Argyris[18] defined different levels of learning/change. The first order of change and learning is that we discover and correct errors in the existing situation. Can we improve the same activity over and over again? The second order of learning and change is that we try to renew the existing situation. Why are we doing what we are doing? Can we do this differently? Can we renew certain tasks and situations and learn to learn? Or, in this context, should we change our business model? The third order of change and learning is, can we transform our company and business model? Can we completely rethink what we do? Technology that can potentially transform industries and companies is DARQ which stands for *Distributed ledger technology*, *Artificial intelligence*, *extended Reality* and *Quantum computing*[19].

The complexity and uncertainty of the different types of innovation lead to a different change management process. Optimizing the Core innovations are focused on internal improvements or improving existing products. The business unit should execute this type of innovation if they own what needs to be improved. 'Renew' the core innovations are more uncertain; the venture team should bring the innovation to a certain maturity level (big enough numbers that match the profit formula of the company), separated from the core business. However, the core business should be involved in the process, step-by-step, to make integration (in a later stage) go smoothly. Future Growth innovations should be separated from the core business and most likely will become new companies; it is not related to the core business capabilities or strategy.

The resource allocation process is a crucial factor for all projects, especially to make Renew the Core and Future Growth innovations happen. Imagine when a venture needs to scale to become successful and more resources (people and money) are needed.

To make the right resource allocation decisions for innovation initiatives, there should be a single point of contact, the venture board.

3.3 Venture boards – Think and act as an investor

 A relevant tool is the checklist: Corporate startup maturity – metered funding.

To lead the portfolio in an effective way, the establishment of a venture board is crucial. This board acts as internal investors and always has the CEO, CFO and responsible P&L business unit directors as core members. This board is like building a mini venture capital firm inside the corporate.

Investment strategies should be built around growth opportunity areas. There are some four hundred venture firms. So how can any firm develop significant market share? The successful venture firms focus on specific opportunities, which means that several partners work together to help build companies in these domains.

Furthermore, how do venture firms pick their investment candidates? Marc Andreessen from Andreessen and Horowitz, has the *what do the nerds do in the evening and weekends* test. Besides making a living, what these people do in their free time is when things get interesting. It is the same as what Peter Thiel means when he says that he does not invest in trends. Why? Because investing in a trend means you are already too late. What the nerds are working on in their garage on Tuesday evening might be interesting stuff. It is the periphery of the market, the *not yet there* or *still at an early stage*.

The successful venture capital firms have found a way to learn at the pace of the market. This is very interesting because many established firms did not figure that out. In order to achieve the success of the market, corporations have to change their mental models at the pace and scale of the market. They will have to overcome disconfirmation biases and the defensive routines that sustain it.

How do venture capital firms work? For starters, they invest and work with a focused portfolio. They invest in multiple high-potential young companies that can outperform the market. They see these businesses as a resolving portfolio of companies in various stages of development.

Interview with Jeroen van Doornik, partner at Rabo Ventures, a sister company of the Dutch Rabobank. He has a lot of experience in venturing in the growth stage.

How do you determine your investment scope within Rabo Ventures?

Rabo Ventures is a strategic fund and within this scope we can invest. One of the main points is to build the capability to become a digital bank. How can we facilitate this? How can we build solutions for our future clients? What happens in the finance industry is that new companies take one service pillar of the bank and deliver that extremely well. We have maybe a couple of thousand IT people, but they work on a lot of different projects, not just one thing, one product offering. We cannot compete with that.

Fintech is obviously our domain, because it is directly related to our core business; but also agricultural tech, because we are one of the leading players in this domain. Crossovers between these domains are even more interesting. Within the Rabobank we look at different horizons of investments, so one bucket is focused on Future Growth. The problem is that it becomes more difficult to predict the economic upside of these investments. As a strategic fund we don't focus on short-term Optimize the Core business investments. When it comes to innovation that is not the way to move forward. Within the Rabobank this is more in the M&A domain. Our experience as a venture fund is that after multiple seed and series A investments, we start to focus on more of the series B investments. Rabobank experienced seed investments as very labor intensive and with these small teams it takes much longer to actually create and deliver value for the bank. The business has different expectations and needs, when it comes to value creation and the timeframe in which this is possible.

For us an important question is, where do we invest in and what is our role? The focus is more on creating strategic (long-term) value, with series A and B investments. We need to understand how customer needs change and what kind of new (tech-driven) business models are out there. Then we try to invest in the companies that can deliver on this.

How are the collaborations between the big and small companies?

Those scale-ups already have 80 or sometimes 200 employees and they can deliver value immediately. My view on these collaborations is that we cannot leave it to a corporate to operate directly with scale-up companies. There are enormous differences in cultures, processes and people. We don't simply sit 'next' to each other and start working together. In order to manage this properly, we share our data and valuable assets with these companies, let them show how to create value and, in that way, improve our own propositions or build entirely new ones. Within a corporate there is no such thing as an entrepreneurial way of working and you cannot compare the situation with outside entrepreneurs. From my perspective, they are on different planets, the speed of innovation and the culture is so distinct.

When we make an early stage investment and the startup needs to collaborate with a business unit, we've noticed that small companies expect that the big bank can deliver tomorrow, if they ask something today. Most of the times this does not work that way; a corporate has procedures and processes to manage and execute at a big scale. This is the opposite of a startup.

How does your VC team relate to the internal innovation department of the Rabobank?

We have moonshot programs, internal accelerators, ideas can be taken further by internal teams. The question is: what do we do with ideas that have the potential to become bigger? Do we spin them out? Is my team investing in them? Are we integrating it into the business?

We can take these teams into our portfolio, as long as they are compliant with the business requirements. Sometimes we just take the product and look for new entrepreneurs that can lead it, but we also have had some management buy-in, depending on what the original founders want. In general, with entrepreneurs you can move way faster. From my experience, the best working model is to use the assets of the business that grow fast if ideas look promising. For a corporate it is interesting to give the entrepreneur funding if the data around the idea looks promising, let them use the assets of the corporate and grow it big.

At what point do you say: "I will take this idea from a moonshot program"?

There is a stage gate process, with product-market fit and other metrics (revenues etc.). That is the end of the internal innovation program. Then we look what kind of partnership is relevant, based on whether it will provide Future Growth. We also have our other *hygiene* factors: What is the growth trajectory? Who are the team behind it? What is the technology? What did it cost till now? What is the exit strategy? For later stage companies, 'return on investments' is the most important check, just like the CVC's (corporate venture capital) of Intel and Google. Financial success is the most important criteria. This success does not have to come back to our company; it is also possible that the business will have tremendous cost savings. The bottom-line is that the P&L needs to get healthier. We do not finance losses.

How does the reporting line go from Rabo Ventures to the bank?

The fund is reporting to the investment committee of the Rabobank for tickets up to 5 million. When investments get bigger than 5 million, we need to go the board of directors.

How do you govern the company that you invest in?

Many CVC's try to get a majority vote/specific terms in the company. Most of the time, the founders of these companies don't want this or follow corporate processes and rules. On the regulatory aspect, companies of course need to comply. We make agreements with the companies upon how they report progress, how often progress updates should be made and what kind of reporting is necessary. We want it, but the shareholders of the bank also want to see the progress of the investments made. Sometimes we also make an arrangement where we are part of their board. Now we hire a venture partner that fulfills the liaison function between the venture, the fund and the bank and manages the relationship and expectations between each party.

We also bump into the difference between the corporate venture capital arm and the venture capital arm. How Rabo Ventures operates is typical for a VC, but with direct reporting lines to the board of the Rabobank. In that way, there is also not really a difference between CVC and VC, because we are playing the same game.

Do you have early warning signs built into your DNA to select and filter companies?

Yes, absolutely. For me it is very important to understand the ambition of an entrepreneur. What is the end-game? Preferably, I would like to understand this in detail. What is the exit exactly? Where does the exit lead? It may not look important, but this question is the key in scanning and screening of the team. I figured out that when the founder cannot explain this precisely, these trajectories are difficult. The founders that can tell exactly towards what goal they are working, are the ones that we potential-ly invest in. The drive of the founding team is crucial. Why are you doing what you are doing?

In a series A investment, founders are not aware of the fact that suddenly you are also married to the investor and their business model. It is good to think about this upfront. For most founders it is important to think again about: Why are we doing this? What were the ambitions? Then there are other important questions. Is the deck of good quality? Is the storyline clear? Is the required investment realistic? Who are the other investors? In other words, is the story consistent with the funding requirement, the sto-ry line and the roadmap to get there?

The difference between a partnership between a VC or startup and the conventional corporation, is in their approach to organizational design. These financial partnerships reveal how to operate at high levels of effi-ciency and scale while emerging in creative destruction at the pace of the market. Venture capital firms never buy a company to hold forever. They focus on intermediate (four-to-seven year) value creation. In contrast, ac-cording to Foster and Kaplan, corporations concentrate on the very short term (less than 18 months) for operations and the very long term (over eight years) for R&D. Moreover, all private or venture capital invest with an exit-strategy in mind. The management of the company, which receives the investment, knows what it must do in the next years to build the orga-nization, so that it has a long-term value for the next buyer.

A corporation that has innovation and growth as high priority on its agen-da, needs a portfolio with innovative ventures. Some will be successful, some will be a spin-out, some sold and others fail. It is crucial for a 'cor-porate investor' to keep the pipeline full of new corporate startups at the front end and to be supplied with *internal buyers* at the back end, cultivat-ing both simultaneously.

The difference between corporate venture capital and private equity investors[20]

In general, corporate venture capital was born because of the low commercialization rate of Research & Development itself, and the difficulty of developing new important technologies internally. Many corporations have recently risen their spending on venture capital; Siemens and Deutsche Telekom are examples. They, among other companies, sense the potential for financial returns and the strategic growth options that venture capital has come to represent. The investments are still low compared to the average R&D investments. But it is difficult for corporate venture capital to act as a private equity investor for four reasons:

1. Corporations often apply the same rules to their venture capital investments as to their normal investments. For example, no cannibalization, no channel conflicts and no dilution of profit margins.
2. Corporations often require majority ownership, which is contrary to the general style of venture investing.
3. Corporate venture capital groups are often led by individuals without proven venture investing records. These people have strong operating records, almost the opposite skillset.
4. The compensation for the leaders of many corporate venture capital groups is more like the internal compensation structure of the corporation. It is difficult to attract the talent that you need. However, there are exceptions like Cisco, Dell or Intel.

Internal venture boards can be seen as an equivalent of a venture capital board. A venture board is a group of senior executives within an organization that regularly meets to review, discuss, and ultimately fund or kill new growth initiatives within the portfolio. Each venture board in each company works differently, but has in general three tasks to perform:

1. The venture board functions as the single point of corporate accountability for the internal startup teams. The mentor and coach ask critical questions and should challenge the intrapreneurs on whether they really make decisions on validated learning or just weak signals from the market. They are the enabling gatekeepers for the corporate startups, who are making decisions about persevere or pivot.

2. Internal corporate startups can get a lot of pressure from other departments when, for example, the project cannibalizes existing business. The venture board acts as a clearinghouse of information about the startup and its progress for the rest of the company. What happens is that middle management can ask for all kinds of updates, but in general wants to see if they can influence the trajectory of the startup. If the team responds, that executive is a member of the venture board and all questions about progress can be addressed to them, challenging middle management twice, whether or not something is worthwhile pursuing.

3. The venture board is accountable for a proper implementation of the *metered funding* concept. For metered funding to work, venture board decisions should be simple: you'll receive ...x amount of budget and ...x amount of time. The startup can spend the money as it wants, but should be fully accountable for everything that costs money. It should also pay the salaries of the employees in the team, equipment, facilities, etc. Why is this important you might think? Because when you need to think about every penny that you spend, you will think twice before wasting it. It's all about creating a scarcity-mentality.

The venture board setup

Small group, right people. A venture board should consist of six to seven members of C-suite level. The group must be nimble, have the authority to act and project to the organization that the work is not only allowed, but is also highly valued. Let venture boards fund teams and problems, not ideas. It is all based on facts. Venture boards must overcome biases about the *right* answer and use the evidence, uncovered by teams, to make deci-sions. The board should meet regularly, every three months, for example. But when there are more corporate startup teams, the number of meet-ings increases.

Action oriented. Venture boards must take go/no-go decisions at the meet-ing. Requests for follow-ups and additional opinions should be an excep-tion. An internal portfolio manager needs to prepare the venture board meetings so that members feel comfortable making decisions.

No attendance, no vote. Only venture board members in attendance may vote, no delegates allowed.

Investor boards invest in companies based on the principles of *metered funding*, a term introduced by Eric Ries. One of its principles is that when a startup has received funding, the money is theirs. Founders can spend it (with minimal oversight) how they think it needs to be spent. But when they need more investments and they did not make progress (validated learning), it is almost impossible to receive extra finance.

3.4 Metered funding

In order to really understand the concept of *metered funding,* it helps to put the general budgeting cycle of corporates next to it. There is an annu-al appropriation process in which all proposed projects, departments and initiatives are evaluated; some projects undergo quarterly adjustments, receive funding and acquire targets for the upcoming years. When things are not going well (economically), it might happen that budgets are taken away, because resource allocation can be readjusted. This system implies that managers need to prepare these annual meetings and need to spend time defending their position.

A lot of politics goes on around the allocation of resources and if your project gets funded, a dysfunctional dynamic can occur. The need to make it successful is huge, because you will be funded year after year, even when it's obvious from a mile away that it will be a disaster. However, to avoid public failure, the project is less likely to get killed, a phenomenon Eric Ries calls *entitled funding*. When you are entitled to get funding, the drive and focus that startups require will be missing. Nobody puts you under resource or time pressure. Innovation without constraints is no blessing.

I remember board meetings where project managers deliberately tried to postpone deadlines, because this way a catastrophic failure could be avoided and there is more time to make the product better. The project manager buys himself more time and gets promoted to another job, while the successor has to deal with the mess left behind. Be careful when people ask you to take over a project, before you know it, you signed up for the end of your career. It is hard to change this way of working. The core problem is the modus operandi for allocating resources, and the power of hierarchy is directly linked to this process.

The antidote for this kind of resource allocation is *metered funding*. The difference is that once you receive funding, there is no way that somebody else will try to take it back. The money is yours. But when you want to have more cash, you should meet some very strict criteria to unlock more funding. Another important difference is that the progress is based on validated learning: you need to validate your riskiest assumptions in the market. You will not receive funding when you do desk research or focus groups. The data must come from the market, retrieved in a scientific way (research validation and trustworthiness). The venture board is accountable for the right execution and implementation of the process of *metered funding*.

Getting funded is the number one priority for innovators with a good idea. As a result, most research about raising capital is focused on how to get it and in such a way that control isn't lost completely. Although this advice is useful, it skips an issue that is potentially more important. The *type* of money that corporate executives provide for new-growth businesses, as well as the type of capital that managers of those businesses accept, can greatly affect the outcome of the idea. Clayton Christensen introduced the 'good vs bad' money perspective. Bad money, in the context of Lean Start-

up activities, is the kind that wants to become big very fast. Because of
this dynamic, companies cannot chase smaller opportunities today that
will become the big ones of tomorrow. It is the perspective of big strategic
plans and annual budget cycles. Good money means that investors give
a little bit of money and ask the team to go into the market and figure
out if and how it works. If teams get too much money, they will have the
opportunity to follow the wrong strategy. Good money necessitates keeping fixed costs low, getting into the market and figuring out what the right
strategy will be. If the strategy is found, then the bigger investments are
legitimate.

 *See the checklist Corporate Startup Maturity – metered funding, to get
an indication of when you are allowed to move forward in the innovation
process, which criteria should be met and what kind of funding is
appropriate.*

Benefits of metered funding according to Eric Ries:[21]

- Scarcity.
- Changes the calculus of who's to blame if a project fails.
- Allows managing a set of projects as an explicit portfolio, along with
  portfolio metrics.
- Greatly reduced political burden on the team.
- Greatly enhanced focus on "What do I have to learn in order to unlock
  more funding?"
- More conducive to cross-functional collaboration, because everyone is
  paid from a common budget.
- Reduced middle manager interference, because no resources are bor-
  rowed from the parent company.

Metered funding is connected to an internal innovation process and innovation accounting metrics, which I will describe in the chapters entitled
Corporate Venture Building and Growth Accounting.

In order to make the venture board meetings more effective, analysis is
separated from decision-making. To make this happen, data that the start-

up teams deliver is validated and analyzed by a business portfolio team. Based on the analysis of the portfolio, the team should create 'what if' resource scenarios and determine project priorities. What if a team finds a product/market fit and we need to double down on investments in people and money? Are we prepared to do this? And what is the effect on the core business?

In any meeting that needs to be effective, make it clear upfront what subjects are going to be discussed. Which milestones do we hold the startup accountable for? Venture board meetings are for making decisions, and not for evaluation or review of funding or stage gate performance.

One of the big FMCG (fast moving consumer goods) companies we worked for, was starting to scale-up their innovation activities internally. At one point they had nine teams running in parallel with different maturity levels. Some were early stage corporate startups, others had already built a minimal viable product and had good traction on their revenue model. The business model worked. With a couple of teams, more serious investments needed to be made. The leader of the innovation engine was part of a two-man investor board, which consisted of himself and the COO of the business. The teams pitched what they had learned and validated, but more importantly, how this might translate into future euros. Part of the governance model was a flexible team, which consisted of people with special expertise (supply chain, branding) that could help the corporate startups in their scaling process. Next to that, important stakeholders were organized in a so-called advisory board. These were the senior managers, responsible for the resource allocation process of the startups.

Venture board maturity phases[22]

"We need to try something new"

At the earliest stage, a company starts with the realization that what has worked in the past, perhaps for many years or decades, might be producing diminishing returns, or even negative performance. We live in a world where customer preference, means of distribution, and capabilities of technology evolve rapidly – and the chances that even a great executive team could be caught by surprise in the throes of a paradigm shift, are high. It is happening all around us, and identifying this moment is the first step in avoiding the fate of the last CEO of Kodak or Blockbuster.

Key Behaviors:
- Acknowledge the need to experiment with new models.
- Identify areas of focus, where the company is prepared to invest.
- Begin to rally behind a couple of internal projects that could be bigger, if managed differently.
- Begin working with an advisor or firm that can bring external perspective to the board.

Expected outcomes:
- Friction between senior leaders, who may see this as an encroachment on their turf.
- Excitement from senior leaders, who see the possibilities of sponsorship.
- Apprehension from some on the uncertainties inherent in such an activity.

Key activities:
- Train the venture board members in the basics of innovation accounting and different types of metrics.

"Let's give this a shot"

Once the decision has been made to start exploring new businesses and new models, an executive team will quickly discover that there's a fair amount of work to do in order to be appropriately thoughtful and rigorous about their new role as investors. Being an investor is notably different than being an operator, and making the best use of the time and perspective of the minds around the table, doesn't always fall magically into place. Allowing appropriately wide and deep consideration of the areas within and outside of the current business, takes research and analysis. The group is likely thinking about the new hires or work reallocation it would have to do in order to run a strong program.

Key Behaviors:
- Run the first couple of board meetings.
- Start collecting the existing internal projects that might merit management through the venture board.
- Start thinking about sources of funding, most often from existing P&Ls.
- Begin to think about the new vocabulary and stage gates that net new businesses are evaluated by (See the venture building process in Chapter 4).

Expected outcomes:
- Rapid progress from the first few teams, especially if they have been freed up and given guidance to chase down new opportunities.
- Excitement from project-team level employees, in a way typically not seen with work within the business.
- Apprehension from P&L ownership on how or whether this new activity affects their goals.
- Discovery that there are likely more *side projects* than anticipated hiding in the organization.

Key activities and questions:
- Formulate the growth gap – can we set as a board a clear revenue number, so the innovation department has a clear goal to achieve?

- Are the innovation projects big enough to bridge the growth gap and well-distributed among the three different kinds of innovation (Optimize the Core, Renew the Core and Future Growth)?
- Does the portfolio as a whole match the growth gap?

"We're starting to get it"

With an innovation team up and running, a list of initiatives gaining increasing clarity on stage gate and resource consumption, and perhaps a string of investment committee meetings, the group has normalized roles. Some of the people present at the start may have fallen off, deciding that their business unit responsibilities are more pressing. In cases where there's a ton of underlying activity, the innovation team should push to organize and prioritize the work, so that the group can better see patterns where they exist. As the board gets more comfortable hearing pitches and disbursing metered funding, it is likely that it has also grappled with the death of previously promising initiatives. Some amount of maturity is starting to set in.

Key Behaviors:
- Full list of internal initiatives scoped and captured; updates to active teams being captured.
- Initial attempts at reporting on the activity coming together.
- Sponsors getting coached up, and facing the friction inherent in week-to-week oversight of explorative teams vs active businesses.

Expected outcomes:
- Starting to see the patterns of what differentiates teams and team members who thrive under conditions of exploration.
- Grappling with questions around career and internal political impact of innovation work at board scale.
- Ability to compare for the first time, investment levels and trajectories of efforts from around the business.

Key activities and questions:
- Where do we see portfolio gaps?
- How is our portfolio helping the company achieving its strategic goals?
- Are we considering *disruptive innovations*, or are we placing *safe* bets that are less innovative?

"Tackling build vs buy vs partner"

With a solid program in place, and active learnings coming back against solid, tested, investment theses, a board is quick to realize that organic bets are not the only way. There are likely terrific vendor companies that could be included in experimentation as a partner, and there are very often small or startup players with tested product or distribution – that the company is in an advantaged position to diligence. The world is opening up to the board, and increasingly, venture board meetings feature buy and partner opportunities that grow out of solid, already validated metrics from organic work.

Key Behaviors:
- Identification and focus being created around intentional investment theses.
- Strong learning through multiple bets in a space. Understanding of key patterns around customer acquisition, product distribution, and other metrics that matter.
- Inorganic bets start getting into the innovation team's tracking spreadsheet, and routinely consider partner relationships alongside their build efforts.
- The company has found ways to fund these bets outside of operating P&Ls.

Expected outcomes:
- Accelerated learning through build / partner or build / buy patterns.
- Strong institutional knowledge in chosen investment thesis areas.
- Sponsors are starting to be subject matter experts and their network is starting to extend to startup founders, ecosystem companies and active investors in their thesis areas.

- As more teams have had more marinating time, the frequency with which new business launch increases, and the activity is very exciting for the company – even for those not directly involved in new ventures.

"Returns are coming home"

Typically two to three years into diligently running and administering such a program, the board is starting to see real outcomes. If we had chosen good theses, we likely have three to four real businesses generating real returns. We might be working on, or may have closed, one to two meaningful acquisitions. The program office's team might be ten to fifteen people, and is working actively with teams, sponsors, and outside parties to organize a diligent and intentional effort on sourcing and research.

Key Behaviors:
- Innovation team has the full confidence of the company and run point on new ventures, investment theses, and acquisition targets. Their insight is golden.
- Board members are rock solid on their chosen opportunity areas and can vet new talent and opportunities with their pattern matching.
- New partnership and acquisition opportunities are inbound as the group's external reputation would be well-established.
- Real financial objectives are being achieved and the program office's P&L ranks with other business units.
- Good talent sticks around or is inbound as the structures and incentives the company would have had to put in place are appealing to builders.

Expected Outcomes:
- Having cleared the J-curve, returns are coming in and are measurable.
- There's line of sight to multiple new businesses that could clear internal targets (typically line of sight to $50MM+ revenue).
- New capabilities are installed and in active use, typically DTC execution, ecommerce, some technical development and more.

Key activities and questions:
*   Is the organizational alignment (especially the resource allocation) from C-level to business unit leadership managed well?
*   Where do we see internal areas of tension?
*   How do we manage these?

"Capability installed"

The venture board is running as a mature capability. The board members relish their roles and see the importance to their jobs and to the company's trajectory. The heads of the board routinely use executive sponsorship as a way to test the ambidextrous skillset of their top executives. The company is living in Day 1, which is the terminology Jeff Bezos uses to describe a company that is always innovating on new horizons and never let status quo kick in.

Key Behaviors:
*   Active allocation of venture fund and active participation as equals, with the top venture investors and entrepreneurs.
*   Board members routinely find themselves coaching their executive peers at other companies.
*   The fear and uncertainty of the activity has gone away, along with the doubts inherent in a *new way of working*.

Expected Outcomes:
*   The company is a leader in their chosen areas and iterating so quickly, it is seen as uncatchable by competitors.

3.5   Resource allocation process

"If you want to understand a company's strategy, look at what they do, not what they say they will do." – Lee Thayer

Strategy is not an event but a process. Strategy must evolve to remain relevant in our ever-changing world. The resource allocation process will determine which initiatives get funded and are implemented, and which are denied resources. And what happens most through the financial system of an organization, resources will flow to the projects with highest *return on investment.* This means that resources will go there where on the short-term money can be made. Despite the existing strategic plans and reports telling that the company should invest in particular Future Growth markets, this is often not the case. If you want to know what the strategy of a company is, don't listen to what board members or management say, but observe what they do.

Strategy is determined by what comes out of the resource allocation process, not by the intentions and proposals that go into it. Leaders who hope to manage the strategy process effectively, need to cultivate a deep understanding of its workings. Many companies don't realize that their own processes are preventing their organization from pursuing innovative ideas.

Good, emergent ideas often come from lower-level employees. Implementing processes to surface these ideas is critical. The strategy that made you successful does not have to be the strategy that keeps you successful.

To make impact: When growth opportunity areas are defined, make an analysis of the current funnel of projects on strategic relevance (growth opportunity areas) and allocated resources. This will lead to understanding how resources are allocated in relation to the strategic goals. This can be very insightful and will help to get resources assigned to your new portfolio of ventures.

In the next chapter we will talk about building new ventures within the corporate.

Points to ponder

"Lots of companies don't succeed over time. What do they fundamentally do wrong? They usually miss the future." – Larry Page, co-founder of Google

Start investing in new business models when the core business is still strong. If you try to get the core business to go after the new one, you will mess up a good business. But if you wait until the disruptive business is dominant, the core business will be atrophied to the point where you have no resources available after this.

When you're looking for new growth opportunities, start with a cost structure in which attractive profits can be earned at low price-points, which can then be carried up-market. Being in a disruptive position relative to competitors, so that they are motivated to flee rather than to fight, will help you more than starting bloody wars with big companies in the same market. Another point to start at are customers, who have been non-consumers and are pleased with modest products; target a job that they are trying to get done. Have the flexibility to respond as a viable strategy emerges and start with capital that can be patient for growth.

Clayton Christensen gives us some guidelines to use, when trying to get disruption to work in your favor:
- Disruption is typically an opportunity long before it's a threat.
- You must begin to innovate while your core business is still strong.
- Allow disruptive businesses to run independently from the core business.
- Spot disruption by observing customers at the bottom of the market.
- Protect your business by focusing on and integrating around the *job to be done* (a topic introduced in the next chapter).

Because in most companies resources (money and people) are allocated to projects with the highest return on investment, innovation is not automatically funded and sourced appropriately. To manage the resource allocation, a venture board that works according to metered funding principles should be installed. This is a group of senior executives (per business unit) that protect the innovative ventures from being disrupted by the core business and the group makes sure, that when the project hits its milestones, it will not dry up because of a lack of resources.

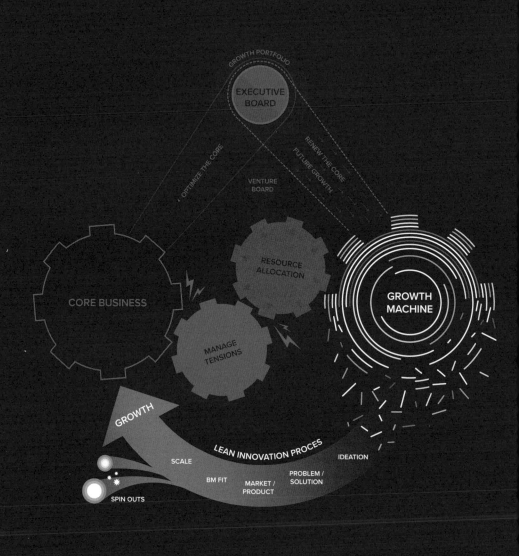

GROWTH PORTFOLIO

EXECUTIVE
BOARD

OPTIMIZE THE CORE

RENEW THE CORE

FUTURE GROWTH

VENTURE
BOARD

RESOURCE
ALLOCATION

CORE BUSINESS

MANAGE
TENSIONS

GROWTH
MACHINE

GROWTH

LEAN INNOVATION PROCES

SCALE

IDEATION

BM FIT

MARKET /
PRODUCT

PROBLEM /
SOLUTION

SPIN OUTS

Chapter 4
Corporate Venture Building

How do we build startups in a lean and mean way in the corporate ecosystem? In this chapter, we discuss the science behind corporate venture building and introduce an end-to-end innovation methodology to ideate, validate and scale corporate startups, with transparent investment milestones per stage. This methodology allows the venture board to evaluate the progress (in and external) startups are making, and prepare for funding appropriately. We'll explore how this works in a corporate setting and present the building blocks for a repeatable methodology for corporate growth. We also touch upon the areas of tension that arise in the corporate when teams start working on new business propositions in a Lean Startup way.

The most obvious outcome for corporate innovation can be defined as a low return on investment. Though most innovation is pursued to provide new income streams. Most corporates lack a space in which existing rules can be broken and innovation will always be compared to existing baselines. New (long-term) growth does not come from product innovations (Optimize the Core), but from disruptive business model innovations, where there is no internal baseline for comparison and forecast.

The 10x Growth Machine Methodology provides a framework with building blocks (strategy and portfolio, end-to-end process, Growth Accounting and venture boards) that allows for re-entry into the organization, assess from an investor's perspective the initiatives in the playing fields (Renew the Core and Future Growth), but also on corporate margin rules (Renew the Core and Optimize the Core). This methodology solves a relevant question for most corporates with existing products: "How large can we grow with our existing range of products if we can enable current market channels?"

Usually, Research & Development does not have the capability to commercialize their technological inventions. Huge sums of money are spent to build dedicated vehicles to win the innovation race.

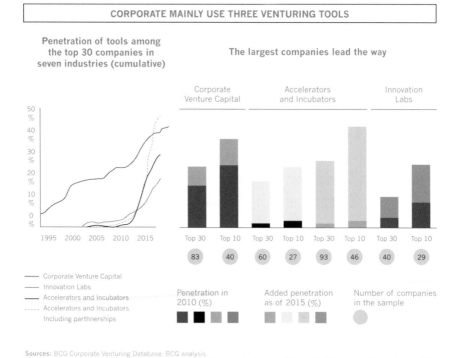

Figure 4.1 – Corporations mainly use three venturing tools

But what are the outcomes of all of these activities? Several big companies shut down their labs. Coca-Cola's Founders Initiative (*shut down* in 2016), Adecco's Ignite Lab (*shut down* in 2016), Disney's research lab (*shut down* in 2016). What are the main reasons for accelerators and venture labs to shut down their operation?

4.1   What problem should corporate venture building solve?

In order to be successful, venture-building initiatives should cover three key topics for a corporate. Dealing successfully with these topics aligns the innovation initiatives with governance practices from the corporate and creates an environment for the innovation projects to operate similar as venture capital:

1. Create predictable timelines for go-to-market of new ideas (small to big) with different phases and milestones. In this way, a corporate can measure its investment readiness of the corporate startup from idea to success.
2. Corporates need big revenue numbers (size of the opportunity) to allocate resources for projects. Arguing that small numbers should be expected, can be difficult with shareholders breathing down your neck. So corporate ventures should be able to forecast the scalability potential of ideas, for the immediate and near future.
3. Forecasting should involve the possibility of existing channels and corporate startups should be able to leverage the existing channels when ready to scale.

The promise of the methodology is to deal with the growth dilemma discussed in Chapter 1. Innovation, when correctly executed, brings huge gains. However, the problem is that these innovative ideas always start small and stay small for a more extended period of time. Nespresso, for example, was not profitable for many years. In corporate politics, small numbers and financing losses is not the way to get promoted.

How venture building should solve these issues

The urge and habit for 'being in control' is a strong force in corporates. This is precisely why corporates in general do not truly embrace innovation. Innovation by nature is uncertain, but can be more predictable if there is the right end-to-end process in place, with timelines per phase. Next to timelines and steps, there is the part of defining the metrics for success. How do we measure our innovation initiatives? The metrics part should keep everybody with both feet on the ground and provide input on the size of opportunity at any moment during execution. In this way, the corporate venture team can counterbalance emotions and opinions with data. Innovation without clear goals and ambitions is doomed to fail. With startup founders, those who know exactly what they want to achieve and why, will succeed over the ones who don't know. Within the corporate context, the biggest threat for emerging markets and rising startups is when corporates start leveraging the scale they have. In other words, anybody can ideate and grow the initial stages of an idea, scaling these ventures is only given to a few companies. To leverage the existing scale corporates that have startups should always build for an exit, spin-in or spin-out. For both the team and the company, the objective is to add value to the company. The exit needs to be clear from the start, so everybody is on the same page about:

1. How success looks like in the corporate context.
2. How to measure this.
3. What the exit plan is.

What the methodology behind venture building doesn't solve is the mindset for innovation. This can only be done through training, execution (running or participating in a venture program) and venture boards. What venture building should do, is provide clarity on process and method of execution.

In general, any idea can be launched in the market with variable success, but we should search for the ones that are scalable and could be the 100 million (new revenues) for the corporate. Venture building is thus an activity in itself that allows companies not only to develop, but also to scale ideas. Venture building is the search engine that is loosely coupled with the mothership for money, resources and channels. The environment allows for creativity without rules and regulations, but the premise is to create the new growth models, not to become a startup founder per se. In this way the culture should differ from regular startup accelerators. It's not about the team on a mission to find a product, but about finding a product with a team. The subtle difference is that we need corporate resources for knowledge and access to channels, but we should complement it with the right growth team for speed of execution and entrepreneurial mindset. Corporate staff, in this sense, is included with the exit in mind. By working in venture building programs, the corporate employees will understand what it means to work in an entrepreneurial manner. Learning by doing, where the ones that understand it will become the next intrapreneurs.

4.2 Way of working: Connect disruptive strategy with Lean Startup and Growth Hacking

A lot has been written already about the Lean Startup, so it is not my intention to write about it again. The same goes for Growth Hacking. Sean Ellis and others have written some great stuff about it.

Instead of the linear product development methods, business plan writing and long budgeting cycles, there's another way to drive change within an organization. A way that is fast, energetic, effective and uses 60% to 80% less time and money. Trial-and-error is a better option than focusing on pure strategic planning. Design and Lean Startup thinking ensures that the process of trial-and-error correction happens before, not after, implementation. This process is critical today, since research shows only 10% of all new product launches succeed.

While a planner may think he already knows the answers, a searcher will admit he doesn't know the answers in advance. Planners trust outside experts and searchers emphasize prototyped solutions. Where strategic plans are based on a presumption of knowledge, searching is based on a presumption of ignorance. Most organizations have a mix of planners, searchers and everything in between. But the reality is that the resources, devoted to plans and planning, vastly exceed those for hypothesis and experimentation. This becomes a costly endeavor when only a tiny percentage of product launches go well.

When a company incorporates the resources for experimentation, the opportunity for discovery and new ideas increases exponentially. Intrapreneurs accept the possibility, even the probability, that what they learn might change their minds and direction. Unlike comprehensive plans designed to address every contingency in advance, there's always another hypothesis to test. When considering bringing an innovation initiative to your organization, keep in mind that the goal is to bring new ways of thinking into the business planning process; to pull together thinking and doing. Experimentation and trial-and-error will play a significant role in strategy development and the teams, who are working closely with your customers, will have the most to offer in terms of direct feedback and customer insights.

In the Lean Startup and Growth Hacking, data plays a crucial role. The venture board is the governance vehicle to test and challenge the teams. Is the problem validated? What kind of data do you have on customer acquisition? The venture board also functions as a link between the operational level and the strategic level. The corporate startup teams should build a business case (Excel sheet) with bottom-line numbers on market size, cost of acquisition, revenue streams, (fixed) costs, etc. The idea is then to prove that there are leading indicators, which show growth when the numbers play out on a bigger level. With Growth Hacking a standard model is the *AARRR framework* (which stands for acquisition, activation, retention, revenue, referral). As an example, to build a healthy (sales) strategy based on the AARRR framework for any particular business model, we need to calculate the cost of acquisition per customer and try to get it down by doing a lot of A/B testing and funnel optimization. Imagine that you identified a disruptive opportunity, but a particular customer group does not buy the new product for premium prices (overshooting). We can target these people and show them multiple propositions to learn how they convert to the new proposition. Understanding growth potential for new or existing products can become evident, way faster than was possible ever before, weeks instead of years.

4.3 The startup journey

In essence, every startup has an identical growth path. One team can go faster because of the product they have or the team that executes, but they cannot skip one of the phases. If they skip a phase, they will die trying, also called pre-mature scaling. Then the question is, how to determine when startups are ready for the next stage. Alistair Croll and Ben Yoskovitz distinguished in their book *Lean Analytics,* five different stages describing the emotional attachment of the consumer with the product in a quantitative and measurable way. These stages are called: Empathy (get to know the customer, their problems and how to solve it), Stickiness (will customers repeatedly use the product or service?), Virality (the product or service provides the functionalities so that it grows organically), Revenue (scalable business with the right revenue model and margins) and Scale (how fast can we grow?).

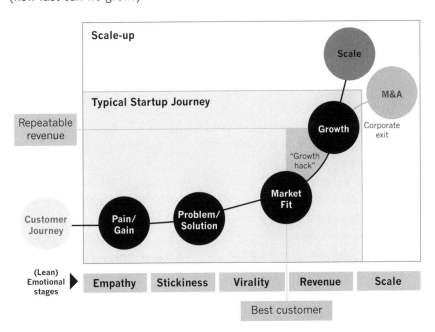

Figure 4.2 – Startup growth phases

With this Lean Analytics framework, we can create a baseline of performance to determine if the startups make the right progress and if they can move to the next phase. It also helps us to actively and precisely steer and influence the growth trajectory (increase speed) of the startup. This growth trajectory is not only relevant for startups but especially for corporate startups. These corporate initiatives cannot make shortcuts and need to work through the same stages to create and launch a successful product of service. The big difference between an external startup and a corporate startup is funding and distribution. Essentially, a corporate already has liquidity and possible distribution, but not an idea, whereas a startup has an idea, but does not have distribution and funding. Marc Andreessen from VC firm Andreessen Horowitz formulates it as follows: "The race between non-digital incumbents and digital challengers is one where the challengers try to achieve critical mass in customer access and data, and the non-digital incumbents try to innovate the business model. Incumbents win if they get innovation before startups get distribution."

If the right team is in place and a precise governance model is implemented, a corporate startup can focus on building the product that trumps customers' expectation and fits within the strategy of the firm. A corporate has a unique set of assets (Marketing, Sales, Logistics, R&D) that makes it possible to go to an exit fast, because there is already scale. Especially when we understand how to make the revenue model repeatable. Corporates have scale, they need to master the art to innovate fast.

Principles of venture building:
- Any startup scales in certain steps (see figure 4.2), where each stage represents an important proof point for the ability of a product to survive.
- Speed of innovation is determined by the quality of the team, execution, money and approach to innovation as a science instead of art.
- Corporate venture building should replicate this startup process and condense the timelines for success given that money, skills, and channels are available. But nonetheless, we should go through the same stages to grow and reach scale. With these principals we can make it sustainable and measurable.
- At the same time, venture building should be flexible enough to change

the flow of the program to counterbalance the nature of the type of innovation (Optimize the Core, Renew the Core, Future Growth). Sometimes markets are already there, sometimes we try to re-segment the market and sometimes we want to grow a new market. All three types require a different execution of the (Lean Startup) innovation process.

In the next paragraph we connect the startup journey with an end-to-end innovation process.

4.4 End-to-end innovation process

There is extensive literature written about growing and scaling startups. The most influential ones are Lean Startup (process) and Lean Analytics (measure). Our challenge however, is that these methodologies do not account (enough) for when you hit the scale stage, nor do they account for corporate restraints.

Traditional stage gate approach for corporate growth

When we understand the process of creative destruction, we understand that the idea is not to control it and completely shut it down by a heavy stage gate process. This may sound obvious, though many companies have such procedures in place for innovative projects. There are careful stage-gates, rapid iterations, and checks and balances built into most innovation processes. Risks are carefully calculated and mitigated. Principles, like Six-Sigma, have pervaded innovation process design, so we have precise measurements and strict requirements for new products to meet, at each stage of their development. From the outside, it looks like companies have mastered an accurate and scientific process, but for most of them innovation is still painfully hit or miss. What's worse, all this activity gives the illusion of progress. The number of committees needed to check the paperwork, going through pitch rounds and business plans, is not the way to compete in highly competitive markets.

Such processes are deliberately constructed to accelerate innovation in the company (though with a different effect) and according to Steve Blank, can be blamed on three mistakes:

1. Too often people think that innovation is an undisciplined and unconstrained bunch of activities and needs to be regulated. In reality, innovation can only move the needle for corporations or government agencies when it is designed in an end-to-end process, from ideation to deployment.
2. Technological advancements that companies may have now, can be easily undermined. Nowadays, new threats appear faster than ever. Existing corporate processes cannot deal with a high speed of change.
3. There is no formal process that supersedes funding and resource allocation. Approvals depend on the best pitch, slides, or the guy that had most friends internally. The problem with this is that there is no incentive for innovators to come forward with proof. Talk to customers, validate problems, build prototypes and actually get market validation and data behind the pricing model before handing over funding.

Before investing time, money and people, you need a way of working in which small ninja teams go to the market and get validations around the most critical assumptions of the new business model. And these teams share their findings with internal investors, gathered in a small venture board that makes decisions based on the data, and the internal prioritization based on the portfolio of projects. Before something goes to an engineering department, we already want a working prototype, tested and based on validated customer needs. The exact product feature set should be known and based on customer data. Companies need an end-to-end process, where progress is self-regulating and data-driven that funnels the innovation portfolio.

If we look closely again at how startups grow and the stages we use to measure progress, linked to the investment tactics of the startup ecosystem, there is a repetition in the way it works. Using the findings, resulting from years in the trenches of corporate and startup innovation, we created a methodology that is repeatable with the right resources and funding.

In the figure we showed the typical startup journey. In the innovation process we show how a startup should move through different stages, which milestones they need to hit to show real progress and how startup growth is connected to corporate growth.

According to Ulwick, an *effective innovation process*[23] must produce answers to the ten following questions:

Finding customers:
1. Who is the customer?
2. What job is the customer trying to get done?
3. What are the customer's desired outcomes?
4. How do they measure value?
5. Do segments of customers exist that have different unmet outcomes?
6. What unmet outcomes exist in each segment?
7. What segments and unmet outcomes should we target for growth?
8. How should we define our value proposition?
9. What new products must we create?
10. Can we convert these customers to this value proposition?

We added additional questions regarding the business impact of the innovation.

Finding growth:
11. Can we sell it to many of them and more than once?

Finding scale:
12. Can we leverage existing channels and portfolio to make predictable revenue, i.e. *monthly recurring revenue model?*

Finding exit:
13. How to transition to the mothership? Spin-in, independent unit, spin-out?

How much should one invest in the disruptive innovation and the growth portfolio?

I am frequently asked the questions like: how much to invest in the innovation portfolio? How much time, money, teams and ideas should be pushed through the innovation funnel? I always start with some stats depending on the client. Let's have a look at the consumer packing industry. Over the last three years only 3.0% of the $35 billion in net growth in the CPG industry has come from traditional, large enterprise players.[24] That is a small percentage. At the same time, about 30,000 new consumer goods are launched per year and 80% fail. Take a 20/1-unicorn ration to find real, long-term growth, which VC's hold as success ratio for investment. There is a clear mismatch between portfolio and return on investment.

Now, here are some questions to help analyze what a company should invest:

1. Take total R&D spend of the company (between 1% and 3% of top line growth).
2. How much of this spend leads to ...x% successfully commercialized product launches?
3. What is the current growth gap for 2023? How much money needs to be made to move shareholder value?
4. Take a 10/2 ratio to find long-term growth. This means from each ten projects, two will become a mature business.
5. We need to invest ...x% of R&D spend in disruptive innovations.
6. The portfolio should have a project distribution of 50/30/20 balance, on Optimize the Core, Renew the Core, Future Growth.
7. Portfolio consists of ... bets / teams internal and 15x external teams in ...x years.
8. As an investor, each of the portfolios should have a weighted pipeline equaling the growth gap with a balanced set of innovation projects for each stage of growth (exploring to scale).

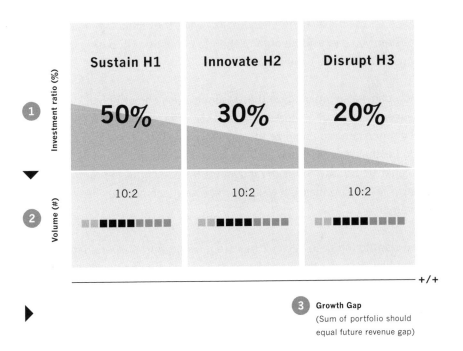

Portfolio
Distribution general / FMCG benchmark

Investment ratio (%)

Volume (#)

①

②

Sustain H1	Innovate H2	Disrupt H3
50%	**30%**	**20%**
10:2	10:2	10:2

+/+

③ Growth Gap
(Sum of portfolio should
equal future revenue gap)

Figure 4.3 – The 10x Growth Machine portfolio

Steps in the innovation process

1. Ideation sprint (1- 3 weeks)

Most big companies have an R&D department full of smart people with lots of knowledge about the latest tech. These guys aren't your regular trend watchers, but most of them are PhDs, so they really know what is technically viable. Challenge these people to select breakthrough technologies and let them explain in plain English what the technology makes possible. Then you can ask the organization to come up with business model options around these technologies.

So how can we commercialize these technologies on our behalf? In my experience, there is not a shortage of ideas in organizations, but it is not for the common good to organize the collective intellect of the organization around a challenge and then actually move forward with some of the ideas in a constructive way. Some organizations have a 'corporate venture capital' arm. If they do their job well, they see new tech and business models in the market.

If you want to innovate beyond the core, dive deep in the periphery of the market and see what kind of companies and business models are in place. Most of the time you will find disruptive opportunities or threats at the outskirts of the market.

Corporate Venture Methodology:
from 0 to scale in 6-9 months

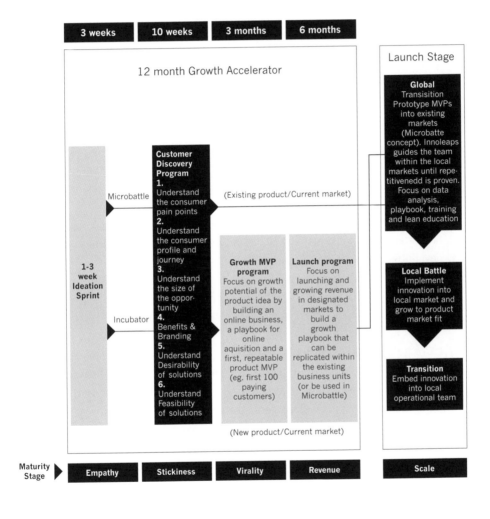

Figure 4.4 – Corporate Venture Model

113

In the 1-3 week ideation program we need to understand the following:

1. Are their ideas worth pursuing?
2. Does the company have a right to win there, based on its existing assets?
3. Is the size of the opportunity big enough?
4. Which critical assumptions are crucial to test first in every idea?

Internal research

It would be smart to do some internal research in larger companies before you step on the gas pedal, so try to answer some of the important questions:

- Where (places) might the problem exist in a slightly different form? Are there any internal projects already in existence? Are there commercially available solutions on the market?
- Have you considered doing a first pro-active stakeholder round to understand possible legal issues, security and support issues?

1.1 Create strategic opportunity areas

If the company has not yet created focus on where the companies want to play, try to narrow down 'strategic' opportunity areas. If the board can align on these areas, innovation gets strategic support, which is very important for innovation teams to be able to survive in the *scaling-up* phase. The board has to commit to these areas and understand that the company is trying to create growth from non-incremental innovation. If these areas are known, it is time to filter and prioritize the first 10 or 20 ideas that go to the customer discovery phase.

2. Customer discovery (10-13 weeks)

Who is the customer? What is the problem they want to have solved? This is the mantra of customer discovery. At the outset, you're spending your time discovering what's important to people and being empathetic to their problems. Right now, your job isn't to prove you're smart or that you've found a solution. Thus instead of developing products, we want to understand the customer. Nowadays it's not about what kind of product to build, but whether somebody cares about your product more than other products. That's why genuinely understanding the customer journey is most essential to finding your Growth Hack.

What I see in big organizations is that they have a product, but they don't understand the customer journey around it, or make the customer journey fit around their product. Why do certain people buy your product? How does that work? How often do they buy it? These big companies are finally becoming aware that they can own the transactions in the whole value chain. If we understand how this customer behaves, we understand what value proposition is relevant and how should we frame it. This in turn determines what we should build first (entire product versus plugin), because based on the understanding of the pains, gains and *jobs to be done* in the customer journey, your entry to market (based on first product features) will become evident. The positioning of the product is then the puzzle between type of market, product and business model.

Key questions for positioning your product:
In the initial stages of a startup we spend a lot of time talking and validating assumptions with potential customers. Most assumptions are based on the pains/gains from the founding team and potentially create a bias. This bias could make it difficult for the startup team to create the right customer segment and product within a timeframe. In other words, wrong questions lead to longer time to market or none at all.

The key to creating pace in corporate venture building is knowing the limits of the innovation targets upfront. Knowing what kind of questions to ask and in which areas – creates focus, the answers create direction.

Questions to answer:
- Who am I competing with?
- Who is the current or ideal target customer?
- What is the unfair advantage?
- What can be key benefits?
- What cannot be built?
- How do we currently measure revenue?

This leads to a first positioning statement (do's and don'ts) and the initial benchmark for profitable growth and input for the metrics model. This generates the knowledge what is good enough and when we should be building for exit.

Positioning Canvas

What is it?	Target Segment
A short statement that describes what you are/do	The specific target market you are targeting in the short term (aka which are the leads you're most likely to close?)
Market Category	**Competitive Alternatives**
Describe the market that you're competing in	If your customers don't use you, what products/services do they use?
Primary Differentiation	**Key benefit**
The one thing (yes, one!) that sets you apart the most from competitive analysis?	The biggest benefit your target market derives from your offering?

Figure 4.5 – Positioning Canvas, source April Dunford, *Obviously Awesome*

Most of the time incumbents already have products, often with declining sales. The key question then becomes: Where in its positioning does the product got off track? Michael Porter coined the term 'stuck in the middle', which means that the product does not really have a big advantage and does not have a beneficial price. In order to understand where in the innovation process the company needs to start, questions around the following variables are essential:

1. Existing product/current market – due to an already existing product and market, we need to spend time re-engineering Who is the customer now? And who isn't? And why? Where do we lose customers and what do they buy now and why? Once we understand this and the results are repeatable in different markets, we go straight to the local market of importance and guide the Sales team on the ground to sell the product in the 'new' way.
2. Existing product/new market – for points 2,3,4 we go after the initial customer discovery phase into a *growth MVP program* to be followed up by the *launch program*.
3. Current market/new product.
4. New market/new product.

When we try to *fix* a product that is already on the shelves, the customer discovery goes faster, because we can ask existing customers why they chose to hire or fire a particular product. But we can also ask other people why they don't hire the specific product. This will give us tons of qualitative insights, which we can validate on a larger scale with A/B testing around different customer segments, pains/gains and *jobs to be done*. In that way, through deductive reasoning, we will find the problem in the current positioning of the product or service.

Couple of steps in this phase:
• Let the teams finish their first Business Model Canvas with estimates of the size of the opportunity. This is a crucial part, because the growth opportunity should be big enough in its potential or we should pivot to a more significant opportunity. We skip the storytelling part in the business case, this is an exercise in fiction. The spreadsheet with some precise numbers is crucial, because it also gives a clear picture

of where the experimentation needs to lead (follow the money).

- Let them clearly describe who the customers are, what they think their problems are and let them state all their (risky) assumptions around the building blocks in the Business Model Canvas. What are the pains/gains and *jobs to be done* in the customer group? How does the proposed solution work from the viewpoint of the users? What would the initial minimal viable product – incremental and iterative solutions look like?

Afterwards, the team should go *outside the building* and put their assumptions to the test by interviewing (asking questions about problems, not selling their solutions) people, who they assume to be representatives of their market.

In the meantime, the innovators should begin to build initial minimal viable products (MVP's) – incremental and iterative tests of the key hypotheses. These minimal viable products can be straightforward; the trick is to hack an experiment from which we can get the most learning. Some (corporate) teams find it challenging to think cheap, because they are used to hiring an agency and building the product. To give an example, if you believe chefs need products or services to create consistently high-quality food, you don't have to create a warehouse of products or build a full-blown platform to sell it to them. It does not matter for the chef what the solution is (in what form), he wants his problem to be solved. So how can we test our assumption that chefs would buy quality ingredients to help him or her create a consistently high-quality product?

The test could be targeting chefs through Facebook advertising with the problem in the ad displayed. Want to achieve high-quality food in a consistent way? When they click (problem validation), they will be sent to a landing page or survey, where the solution is described with some unique selling points related to the validated pain points of the customer.

Some ideas will drop out when the team recognizes that some solutions may be technically, financially or legally unfeasible; or they may discover that other groups have already built a similar product.

Portfolio prioritization

When teams are working for a couple of weeks in the customer discovery phase, it is time to check in as a venture board on the progress that is made. Do we kill or adjust the plan? To segment ideas, it is helpful to use the three playing fields: Optimize the Core, Renew the Core and Future Growth. It gives an idea of how to move forward.

1. Optimize the Core: Is about continuing improvements in existing business and capabilities. In many organizations these kinds of innovations are the own responsibility of the business unit.
2. Renew the Core: Business model innovation, ideas extend a company's existing business model and core capabilities to new customers, markets or targets.
3. Future Growth: Is the creation of new capabilities taking an advantage of or responding to disruptive opportunities or disruption?
4. Graveyard: The graveyard is the place where ideas land when they are not feasible or viable.

Don't underestimate the power of the *graveyard*. In many companies (where we have worked) there are no checks and balances that help to terminate projects that are not viable or feasible at an early stage. When the investments get bigger, it becomes more difficult to pull the plug. It is a process that creates dramatic outcomes. The reason for this is that we pull more risky projects in a process that is built to execute projects. Bury ideas that do not work with honor in the graveyard.

3. Growth MVP phase (12-15 weeks)

The ideas that survived the first validation in the market, go to the next phase. In this phase we connect the growth metrics framework[25] (acquisition, attention, retention, revenue, referral) with strategic questions like:

1. How can we attract customers that are not satisfied with existing offerings to our products/services?
2. How can we enter a new market? In this phase, we need to figure

out the route to market (message/market/pricing). The focus lies on the right side of the Business Model Canvas: value proposition (messaging), acquisition channels, customer segments and pricing model.

3. How do we communicate the value proposition and who is it meant for? Which message consistently gets the highest conversion rates? What is the cost of acquisition of getting a new customer in our sales funnel? In this phase we learn to understand the repeatability of the value proposition and MVP adoption.

The growth MVP phase should lead to a product/market fit. This means having the business model validated at a small scale. At this point we have figured out the pricing model, understand why customer groups buy the product (repeatedly, if necessary) and figured out the *growth engine* (viral or paid). The business shows signs that the case (as a whole) is financially healthy. Nonetheless, in this phase a couple of additional checkpoints should be met:

- Hi-fi MVP is built and shipped.
- Annual recurring revenue model is achieved.
- Further investment and implementation plans are ready to integrate in the core business or to spin-out.
- On the business side, it becomes necessary to see which resources and capabilities (R&D, supply chain) are needed to build and scale the product or service further.

Athlon's Strategy = Execution

While traditional corporate planning relies on outside consultants who can take months to years to develop and leave execution to the workforce, the business world is moving entirely too quickly to sustain those practices. Good ideas are never easy or simple to implement, but in order to be flexible and adjust to dynamic market conditions, it is crucial that the teams, working directly with customers, are able to influence strategy.

Athlon is one of the leading providers of car leasing and fleet management in Europe. The first and most important step of starting a (corporate) startup was team selection. It was vital to have at least three types of people on the team: one person who is business savvy (the hustler), one person who is product-focused and usually with more technical skills (the hacker) and one person who is strong in operations and project management (the helper). A balanced team with additional skills and expertise is essential to perform successfully.

The team entered an Ideation Sprint. Spending time diving into their assumed customer challenges, Athlon developed a long-term goal: "A simple and flexible mobility solution with an excellent digital experience and maximum transparency"; and a sprint goal: "Focus on a simple and flexible car (lease) product".

After defining the sprint goal, the team went through the process of ideation, prototyping and testing. They prototyped an app, which solved the problems underlying the sprint goal, and showed it to customers during customer interviews. They found out that the common challenge in all customer interviews was the problem of a long-term (typically five years) fixed contract. Their new solution was far more flexible.

Shortly after the ideation sprint, the team entered the next phase in the innovation process – a 13-week Growth MVP program with the goal to find an idea/market fit with proper validation of the prototype and revenue model. The first weeks were heavily focused on customer validation, to determine their customer and their challenge. The team talked to 25 (potential) B2B customers (employers) and more than 100 end-users (employees) and started experimenting with different solutions. They worked on finding out more about their customers, end-users, their car choice, difficulties and problems. Along the way they shifted from a focus on millennials (B2C proposition) to a B2B proposition with a focus on employers.

After the customer interviews, some assumptions were validated and others were discredited. For example, the assumption that customers did not find car leases transparent was quickly found to be untrue. However, the team did find that customers experienced issues when contracts changed. Once they gathered customer data, the team started running experiments to test their hypotheses/assumptions further. Most experiments they ran were online: setting up Facebook advertisements, LinkedIn surveys and creating their own landing pages.

Once the team found their problem/solution fit, they started building their MVP, an app allowing customers to compare and change their lease car on a monthly basis. During the program, the team worked in two-week sprints, setting short-term objectives and showing their progress to stakeholders on a bi-weekly basis. This ensured the alignment of the team with internal organization as well as transparency of the process.

The real work came when the team started setting up flexible lease products on an operational and logistical level. After researching, they decided to use the Athlon own system and logistics; this was seen as an advantage of being part of a bigger organization.

At the same time, the team began to experience pushback from the Athlon organization due to anxiety about cannibalizing another Athlon car lease product. The teams reaction was and still is: "If we don't build this company, someone else will", which basically raised the question whether Athlon was prepared to cannibalize itself or let another company do that for them. In addition, tensions arose when Athlon's Finance team started asking about the Return on Investment measure. The team's initiate success was focused on different metrics: Can we identify our customer? Can we validate the customers' problem? What is the price? What is the customer retention rate? Their goal was to validate a new business model.

After three months in the program, the team had acquired the following insights:

- *40% of lease car drivers (passenger cars) wanted or needed a more flexible product than their current offering. That equals to 180,000 cars.*
- *80% of current Athlon customers interviewed saw added value of the CMC MVP.*

The team showed their progress and product to their stakeholders and Athlon colleagues. They received an investment for the next six months to develop a beta version of their MVP with a small selection of cars and customers.

Today, the ChangemyCar/Athlon team is ready to enter the market and has the full support of the Athlon Board to do so, and is making more than a million euros annually.

4. Launch program (13-26 weeks)

This program is focused on launching and growing revenue in designated markets. The goal is to build a growth playbook that exactly tells us how to grow the product or service. Another important aspect here is to figure out the operations side of the business in these markets. For example, are partner agreements and local resources in place? Are the margins per sell stable and good? Does the team make money every month in a recurring way? Can we improve the growth rate?

In the next chapter on Growth Accounting we focus on making the growth accountable and transparent. We focus on different types of metrics; introduce a metric model for growth and present real life situations and examples.

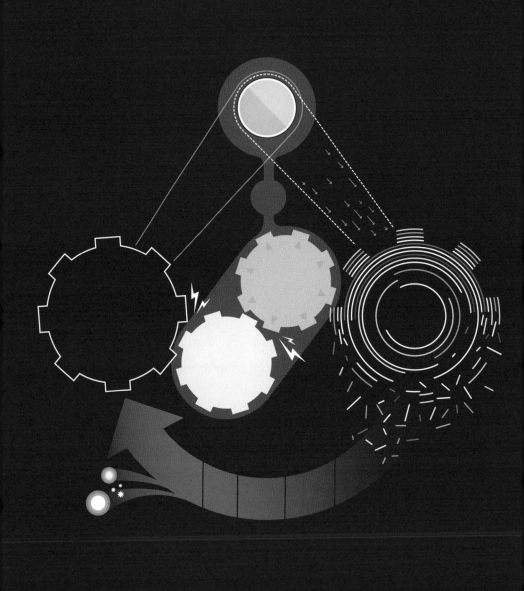

Chapter 5
Growth Accounting

Growth Accounting refers to the rigorous process of defining, empirically measuring and communicating the true progress of innovation – such as customer retention and usage patterns – whether for startup companies, for new products or business units within established companies. The main challenge for corporates that take innovation to the next level is to understand how learning can be translated into euros or dollars and to figure out what the growth trajectory is.

In essence, there are two values of extreme importance, which determine whether projects are funded or not: *gross margins* and *size of the opportunity*. In big companies, the projects most likely to be funded are the ones with the highest or same gross margins as the existing business, and markets with most significant opportunity. This means that initiatives, which do not meet these criteria or cannot show relevant tangible data, will be killed. Related questions are then:

1. How do we measure the progress and performance of early stage (corporate) startups?
2. What does this mean for Future Growth?
3. How can we translate the learning experience into something everybody understands, i.e. money?
4. What kinds of questions are relevant to ask the startup team?
5. What kind of metrics do we use?
6. And last but not least, how do we finance early stage startups appropriately?

Imagine that you are a part of a corporate startup team. Your boss has invested 100k to set up the team for first discovery and validation, and you have the task of finding a new proposition in an existing market. During the first week, you and the team need to get into a very different way of working, but manage to crank up a hundred interviews in order to really understand the problems of the potential customer you have in mind. The first interviews feel awkward, because you do not try to sell anything to the customers. You just want to understand them and, surprisingly, customers share their whole life stories. Back to the story-board. Because of the new insights, you are fired up to create some first solution prototypes. In the meantime, you are observing the client in their own habitat and understand more about the *job* the customer tries to get done, and the pains he experiences in trying to achieve this. Online validation starts with Facebook ads, Google ads and landing pages. You try to figure out how to communicate the different value propositions and which acquisition channel leads to highest conversions. Click-through rates are disappointing. The team starts iterating the messages and re-fines the persona groups. Click-through rates go up. Next step is to start selling the product. Long story short, in thirteen weeks you've figured out what the route to the market is (message, market, pricing) and you managed to sell in one week a total order value of 18,000 euros (this is a food product, so cheap to buy). All passionate about the fact that you cracked the puzzle, you pitch the opportunity, your discoveries and next steps forward to the internal sponsors. You ask for 500,000 euros to scale-up production and marketing spend to ship more products. Though the sponsors are excited, they do not want to give you the 500k. Why is this do you think?

Metrics are critical, because when leadership can't measure results, the common response is to require all decisions to go up to their level. The first-order effect of better measurements is better decision-making. The second-order effect is that leadership gives high- performing teams the autonomy to act faster and focus their attention on the right things.

The point of Growth Accounting is to identify and track leading indicators for Future Growth in a language that financials love. From a change man-agement perspective, Growth Accounting is a highly effective and essential building block of the Growth Machine. Without measuring performance, all opinions are equal.

The terms growth and accounting are both well-defined and understood. However, by combining the two terms together, they take on a very different meaning. Where traditional accounting measures are used to measure innovation, it has the effect of stifling or suffocating the new product or startup company. That means that traditional accounting tends to work best when measuring established products or on-going concerns. By definition, new innovations have a limited operating history, little to no revenue and are burning cash well in excess of revenue. In this context, financial ratio analysis, cash flow analysis and other standard practices shed an unflattering light on the new innovation, especially in comparison with existing products or businesses within established companies.

5.1   How Growth Accounting works

In the 1990's, IBM was confronted with the harsh reality of missing the opportunity to establish early leadership in many new tech markets, from network routers to data communications and the internet.

While there were several reasons for this, one crucial factor was that IBM applied the same rigorous metrics to its new products as it did to its established products, which led them to be discontinued. When Lou Gerstner joined the company as CEO during IBM's darkest days, he recognized that this had to change and he developed the Emerging Business Opportunity Group (EBO), that was in charge of identifying new billion-dollar businesses for IBM. One critical change that Mr. Gerstner implemented was to alter the way the new business opportunities were evaluated.

He brought in entrepreneurial executives to lead these new ventures and tasked them with eliminating market ambiguity and increasing strategic clarity. Ultimately, the IBM EBO approach resulted in a number of new multi-billion-dollar businesses, re-energized and re-established IBM as a major player in the IT space.

IBM was very serious about not missing more business opportunities. They hired experienced entrepreneurs with decision power to explore disruptive opportunities. They had dedicated resources, separate business units to achieve these breakthrough innovations and innovation KPI in exists reporting lines.

Growth Accounting is about having the right metrics to measure progress of early stage ventures. The 'growth' dilemma for established companies is that they need to communicate growth expectation with shareholders. Renew the Core or Future Growth innovations are small today, but can be big in the future. It is crucial to show that if you have the right metrics in place, Future Growth can be identified. As Clayton Christensen says: "We need to be impatient with revenues, but patient for growth". It was widely believed that it takes much more time to grow innovative business models to a big scale. The case in fact is otherwise. Fast disruption happens by building on existing technologies uniquely configured, packaged and/or delivered, and combining them with a *speed of good enough deployment as a force multiplier* mindset. In the commercial space, Tesla and Airbnb are good examples, and the explosion of machine-learning solutions are the examples of radical disruption using existing technologies in concise periods of time.

Imagine the next situation: the board identified a growth gap. You have been assigned to lead a new innovative category with certain growth expectations. The board is impatient for growth. Expectations are high, thus this category should go sky-high. A couple of things might happen when you pitch your progress in the first *venture board* meeting. You pitch about what you have learned, you identified a problem in the market and show evidence that the alternative solutions in the market are not performing great. As an entrepreneur, this is the stuff you get excited about. During your pitch you notice that a couple of board members are checking their iPhones, though they say it is interesting. After your pitch you are questioned about when you are going to bring in the big cash. Are you strong enough as an intrapreneur to tell the board that this may take a while, and that your goal is to validate the business model on a small scale and show leading indicators for growth?

It is crucial to manage these expectations. Talk about the growth dilemma that big companies face and align on the kinds of metrics for success that you will use in the venture board meetings. If you don't do this, you will be pulled into the existing processes of the corporate organization.

5.2   When you don't use innovation accounting

Within a big FMCG company the decision was made to create a product in a new market. The team leader was forced to go with this new product idea through the existing stage gate process suited for product innovations (Optimize the Core). Though people saw the opportunity and were enthusiastic, the business case needed to show big turnover numbers, otherwise the necessary resources would not be allocated. To produce these numbers, the product opportunity was bent towards an existing market in which the figures were known, thereby losing the new-market disruption potential. The big numbers in the business case created a dynamic of too big to fail. That is the worst thing that can happen in a project with a lot of uncertainties in the business model.

Companies lack a de-risking process allowing the plug to be pulled at an early stage of the project. The more time and money spent on the project, the more difficult it becomes to pull the plug. The project team cannot fail and start asking customers if they would buy the product, to create a scenario that looks positive. Though in customer development, the number one sin is to ask people about future behavior, because nothing is more unpredictable. This dynamic creates a system that goes from a positive scenario to a more favorable plan. It becomes a self-reinforcing system based on hallucinations.

When the product was launched, the sales figures were disappointing. The company blames the research party for doing bad evaluation, literally pulling everything new through their existing linear processes. This is the best way to kill disruptive ideas or new inventions. It takes two to three years to get a perfect product on the market. This traditional product development approach takes a lot of time and resources. In the end, the final result does not live up to the hyped numbers. After all, companies create their own disasters by pulling new ventures through existing processes.

5.3   Metrics

The term *vanity metrics*, coined by Eric Ries, are metrics that give you a good feeling, but don't tell you anything about how to proceed. For example, we have 15,000 visitors on our website. Is it good? Compared to what? If you are building a business model based on advertisement income, it may be good or bad, depending on which niche market you are operating. To clarify, vanity metrics do not give *leading indicators* that show us if we are on the right growth trajectory. In many organizations, people are not critical about these kinds of numbers during a presentation.

In the Lean innovation process we make a distinction between *activity metrics* and *actionable metrics*. An *activity* metrics tells us something about what we did. For example, team A validated three hypotheses in two weeks by interviewing one hundred customers. Another activity metrics on a different level is: "How many people in our organization are trained in Lean Startup methodologies?" Companies love to benchmark these kinds of numbers, a well-known R&D spend. But does it tell us anything about the performance of people? And does it show the overall performance of the company?

We distinguish three levels of metrics for a balanced Growth Accounting approach:
- Metrics on the project level.
- Metrics on the process level.
- Metrics on the portfolio level.

In order for this approach to be effective, the different levels need to be connected with each other. In this way, innovation labs can be held accountable for three performance standards:

1. The startup teams in the innovation labs are held accountable for the progress they make in their validation journey (operational metrics).

2. Can the innovation lab measure the performance of the pipeline? How many teams are in a specific maturity level? How much investment did it cost?
3. The innovation lab can translate the progress the corporate startups make or the learnings of the team into a strategic value: "Does the team make progress in gaining a foothold in a new market? Did the team find leading indicators for growth in this new market? If yes, what is the *cost of acquisition* for one customer?"

Next you can see the metric table for Growth Accounting to get an impression of the different kinds of metrics and how the three levels are connected with each other.

Metric board for Growth Accounting

	Activity metrics	Actionable metrics
Strategic	How many patents?	New market share?
	How many poc's?	Is the company achieving growth and productivity?
	How many collaborations with universities?	Is the company delivering for customers in a simpler way?
	How manu people are trained in Lean startup?	Has it become the way working in the company?
	How many leaders bought in to the growth transformation approach?	Cost savings?
Tactical	How many ideas in the pipeline?	How many ideas are the problem- solution fit?
		How many ideas are the product- market fit? How fast? For what costs?
Operational	How many experiments per week?	How many hypothesis are validated?
	How many decisions made?	Pirate metrics
		Conversion rates

Figure 5.1 – Metric Board for Growth Accounting

Metrics model operational level

The biggest challenge in venture building is to overcome the lack of big numbers. With a running business, the tendency of management to discard big ideas with small numbers is very big, if not a fact. When running, venture building metrics are crucial for success, both for the programs and for the idea itself. Aligning growth of ideas with corporate standards is the key to Growth Accounting.

For venture building we shouldn't be focused on the metrics, but rather on what these numbers forecast, especially when forecasting exponential growth. The trouble with building a projection model for future added value is that these start small, and we have to prove early and often that the team is on track.

In order to facilitate this, we created a metrics model, inherently built on multipliers (virality) and works independently from type of business model (Lean Analytics). This metrics model consists of three basic business model metrics, plotted over time.

Key questions:
First, we focus on business model metrics. At any given stage a startup should be able to provide an answer to the following questions:

1. Market: What is my Market? Do potential customers experience pain that gives us a right to play? And how many of them are there?
2. Product: Through which business model can we deliver? Can we develop a product that solves a problem AND fits existing channels?
3. Method: How should we approach the market? Can we create a methodology that converts these customers into consumer? Repeatedly? And for the right price?

Metric Multipliers

We can collect data separately for each of the business model metrics and benchmark with metrics. However, this does not account for a growth engine. Just think, if we can improve our product but fail to attract a larger audience, what should we do? Does it make sense to continue?

Scale = Product x Market x Method

Innovations that grow the fastest provide answers to all three questions, as these have to be in balance at all times to win and scale. Balance in this case means to provide clarity continuously, independent from business model or product. And therein lies both the challenge as well as the solution.

If we can grow all three metrics at the same time, the multiplier will provide exponential scale. If we can only offer one or two, the issue could be that the product stays small and cannot be leveraged by existing channels.

In order to build a growth engine, we need the combination of these metrics to assess growth potential. If you can improve all three (market, business model, go to market), the results multiply per stage. For example, if we increase retention by 30%, we can hit success. But if we can increase retention AND increase the total number of customers by 30%, we are going viral.

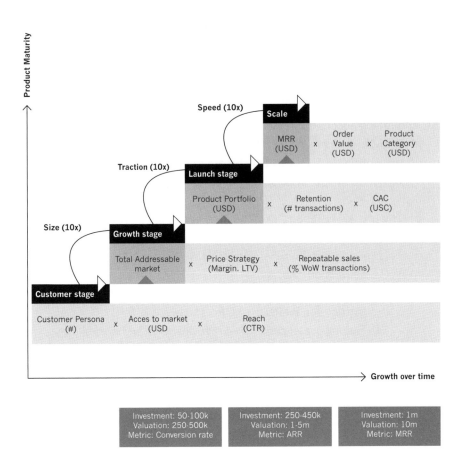

Figure 5.2 – Scale model

In addition, if we create an overall goal of 10x growth per stage, the three multipliers should strengthen each other and stop being a goal by itself. Focusing on the multipliers allows us to show growth per stage and forecast whether we can hit the multimillion-revenue stage the corporate mothership desires.

Benchmarking success is achieved by:
a) Deriving benchmark data from the existing market. With this measuring stick we can benchmark how scalable a product is within existing channels.

b) Treating every venture like investing in a startup. In general, the metrics model provides targets for an exit:
   1. Finding customers: can we convert them? Metric: conversion rate.
   2. Finding growth: can we sell to the many and more than once? Metric: Annual Recurring Revenue.
   3. Finding scale: can we leverage channels and portfolio to make revenue predictable? Metric: Monthly Recurring Revenue.
   4. Finding exit: Transition to mothership, predictable revenue.

5.4   Traps of measuring innovation

Measurement is not a topic to think about lightly, because the wrong measurements can have serious consequences. For instance, a set of KPI's a manager is rewarded for and thus is measured by, will determine 90% (maybe even 100%) of his agenda. If we measure only output on existing business KPI's, don't be surprised if that innovation comes low on the agenda. Another example is that a measurement can be biased, depending on how we execute it.

It is not my intention to write an epistle around the science and philosophy of knowledge creation, though here I would like to point out some basic pitfalls:

1. People give socially accepted answers. Because social interaction depends on being tactful, relationships work based on a form of hypocrisy. If we tell people the truth (too often) we can end up alone. For example, if you depend on surveys to measure the quality of your programs, there is a strong possibility that people will not tell you the truth. This means that the survey result is likely to be grossly distorted and making decisions based on surveys could be disastrous. In order to avoid making wrong decisions based on false facts, we should combine qualitative and quantitative research.

2. Within many fields of expertise, conducting good measurement and research is a profession. It is not something that is given and effortless. There are many factors that can distort the data. Do you conduct the research anonymously or not?

Knowing what I have seen in practice, here are some common mistakes:

1. *Measure innovation alternatives, not just the current activities*. When assessing the impact of an initiative, always ask: "Compared to what?" Don't fall into the trap of measuring only what the company is doing today. Rather, measure it against the next best alternative.

2. *Measure inputs, not just outputs.* Companies are quick to judge innovation initiatives based on the yield of ideas. A better approach is to be mindful about the company's inputs in innovation. Measure activities such as the number of training sessions conducted, number of employees skilled at a methodology, and man-hours used in innovation workshops. But also, how high the price of fast learning is. Benchmark these against competitors and other relevant companies to create an indication of whether you are investing enough.

3. *Measure quality, not just quantity.* People focus too much on quantitative measures, because they're easier to collect than qualitative ones. Quantitative data seems more objective, though to understand the customer journey thoroughly, qualitative research is just as important.

4. *Measure to improve, not to judge.* Hold people accountable for what they do to improve innovation activities. It is tempting to judge employee performance and reward them for innovation output. This can lead to the unwanted rivalry between employees.

5. *Measure novelty, not impact.* Senior leaders want to know the bottom-line impact of innovation. When they see ideation results, they respond with: "Yes, but how many of these actually made it into the marketplace, and which revenues were generated?" This is a trap, because the impact depends so much on internal and external factors. Holding employees accountable for impact will cause them to avoid the truly novel and game-changing ideas. To manage this dilemma, managers need to think more in terms of finding the *innovation sweet spot*, i.e. a place somewhere between disruptive and incremental. The right balance between risk and reward is more likely to occur here.

6. *Measure future potential, not just past results.* Managers must be forward-looking, so they can spot which innovation initiatives will make the firm more competitive. Measuring only past results is like driving a car while looking through the rearview mirror. Avoid this trap by analyzing where to invest in product, process and service innovation. Quantify the value of innovating in the key areas. This will help you find your leverage points quicker, ahead of the competition.

7. *Measure execution, not just ideation.* Executing and launching new products takes financial and human resources. When poor execution delays a product launch, companies are hit with a cost that is often unnoticed. Poor execution delays the revenue stream that a new innovation will earn. Given the time value of money, the financial loss can be staggering. Avoid this by forecasting the net present value of delayed product launches, then hold teams accountable for that cost when delays occur.

8. *Underestimating or overestimating.* Not everything that can be counted counts, and not everything that counts can be counted. This is the case when companies count metrics that only tell us something about an activity, for example, the website has a 100 million visitors. If you don't have an advertising business model, this number does not tell us anything.

9. *Measuring parts, but not the whole.* Fragmented knowledge can do more harm than good. This is the reason why I make a distinction in this book between *project, process and strategy* metrics. If we only measure the progress of teams, how do we connect it to governance questions like: "How healthy is our innovation pipeline?

Or how many teams in our innovation process are in the product/ market phase?" Or more strategic questions like: "Did the corporate startup actually have paying customers in a new market? What percentage of this new market are we going to capture if we understand the leading indicators for growth?"

10. *Overlooking the political aspect of innovation measures.* What gets measured is what gets done and what gets done is what gets rewarded. Changing the way innovation gets measured implies that some groups or goals will become more important, while others will become less relevant. Sometimes this leads to heated discussions about what gets measured and what not.

To make venture building possible in a corporate setting, we need to manage the innovation function professionally, by having the right organizational model, governance structure and processes in place that enables rapid experimentation and building business in the three playing fields. This will be the focus of the next chapter.

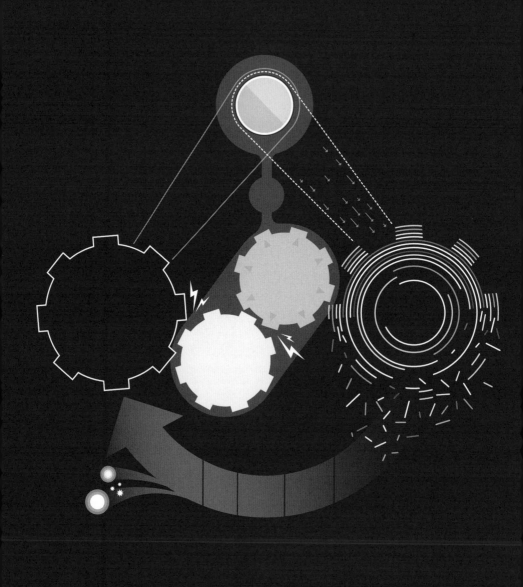

Chapter 6
Innovation management

Innovation is a craft and entrepreneurship – an art. To create something out of nothing is hard work and should be managed. Many entrepreneurs like to go from zero to one. But the main challenge is to go from one to ten thousand. To achieve this, we need to become high performers. However, there are no shortcuts. There are no five or seven easy steps. Becoming a virtuoso at changing the course of things, intervening and putting a person or situation on a better path for everybody, requires more of you than being merely a professional. It is challenging and requires more focus and diligence, just like good management. Intrapreneurs should be artists and scientist, freethinkers and real managers.

In this chapter, I will elaborate on how to organize the function of an intrapreneur in relation to innovation ambitions. What do we want to achieve? How do we organize ourselves for this? The processes of large organizations are not designed to learn fast, but to avoid risk and follow a methodology to create predictable outcomes. When we start working in an entrepreneurial way, tensions will arise between the modus operandi (processes, metrics etc.) of the big company and the small corporate startup. How should we deal with this?

6.1   Corporate startups, a two-front war

"Even validated innovation concepts struggle to get deployed at scale due to two root causes: (a) Lack of connection between innovation venture and core and (b) Lack of an end-to-end process, comprising proper transition of the innovation into the core". – Steve Blank

While external startups might struggle with finding a product/market fit before running out of money, corporate startups are forced to fight on an internal front. Managing the *areas of tension* is a crucial task of each corporate innovation manager and intrapreneur. This tension comes from the different and incompatible designs and operating models of these two organizations, which are based on two distinct rationales. This tension cannot be solved, and it cannot be avoided, but it can be managed.

To get from exploration to impact, tensions along the scaling process need to be managed well. Especially when the integration of innovation teams with the hierarchy is necessary for a scaling trajectory. What I've noticed with many corporate startup teams, that went back into the core business, was that they died slowly by being pulled back into the core. The question then becomes obvious: When is a corporate startup ready to be integrated, or prepared for spin-out?

To achieve success in the market, corporations have to change their mental models at the pace and scale of the market. They will have to overcome the disconfirmation biases and the defensive routines that sustain it. In my previous book, I have already written extensively about how mental models determine how we interpret the world around us, through habits of perception (thinking, feeling), until it becomes a part of who we are. We identify ourselves with the ideas we have, we become attached to them, create emotional reactions around it and defend them when under attack. We try to push and pull new ideas through the same process as simple ideas. We analyze, make plans, have meetings and argue about it. At the same time, we do not validate anything in the market, an approach that makes no sense at all.

Implementing a new way of working is always challenging. Colleagues will argue that it is not possible, that it is too risky and that the planned outcome will not be achieved. What can you do about it? Are you ready to confront your tensions? When you are trying to build new growth ventures, do not expect that the whole organization will be cheering for you. Innovation always creates internal differences. New business dilutes old business and successful innovators can become the future leaders, where others are left behind. You are at war. People will try to talk you out of it, or maybe sabotage it later. Can you deal effectively with this? What would you say to people in a meeting, when for the third time, they have not done what they promised?

If you look at the tasks in hand – Optimizing the Core, Renewing the Core, and creating Future Growth – you can conclude that these are challenging. The threat lies in the fact that we talk about managing two different paradigms at the same time. We want to execute fast, stable, maybe with a sigma score of 0,000043 and making mistakes is fatal. At the same time, we try to create new growth engines that can cannibalize the core. Think of the tensions that can emerge in the organization. Changing the policies, structure and other important factors will not lead to the desired results if we don't deal with the negative emotions or irrational dynamics in the organization. I agree with Foster and Kaplan when they say that the same amount of time should be focused on the internal shift, that what people think and feel, that has to occur, to bring the strategy to life. This is where resistance tends to arise, cognitively in the form of fixed beliefs, deeply held assumptions and blind spots, and emotionally in the form of the fear and insecurity that change generates. All of this is merged in our mind, which reflects how we see the world, what we believe and how that makes us feel.

Transforming a business also depends on transforming individuals – beginning with the most senior leaders and influencers. Few of them, in my experience, have spent much time observing and understanding their motivations, challenging their assumptions, or pushing beyond their intellectual and emotional comfort zones. The result is something that the psychologists Lisa Lahey and Robert Kegan have termed *immunity to change*.

What dominant patterns of thinking, being and doing can be an obstacle for the change the company wants to see? Even if patterns are made explicit, it does not mean that the people in charge (can/want to) change their behavior.

A useful exercise, when trying to understand the irrational (board) dynamics, is to ask people the following:

- Imagine a situation in which you were not effective in achieving your own goals.
- Try to remember a specific moment in the conversation.
- Now grab a paper and divide it into two columns. In one column you write what you said. In the other column you write what you thought.
- How many discrepancies are there between what you say and do, and what you think?

Now that we have talked about the challenges on the human side of venture building, let's dive deeper into the matter.

6.2   Organizing the intrapreneurship function

What is intrapreneurship? Wolcott and Lippitz (2007) define it as: "the process by which teams within an established company conceive, foster, launch and manage a new business that is distinct from the parent company but leverages the parent's assets, market position, capabilities or other resources. It differs from corporate venture capital, which predominantly pursues financial investments in external companies. Although it often involves external partners and capabilities (including acquisitions), it engages significant resources of the established company, and internal teams typically manage projects. It's also different from spin-outs, which are generally constructed as stand-alone enterprises that do not require continuous leveraging of current business activities to realize their potential."

There are many ways to organize corporate entrepreneurship. In most companies there isn't explicit interconnection made between the strategic goals that need to be achieved and the way the innovation function is organized to achieve these goals. Companies have tried to implement corporate entrepreneurship by appointing an innovation leader. Such approaches, however, often failed. It is one thing to recognize "organizational slack" as a critical factor enabling 3M Co.'s success – 3M allowed its engineers and scientists to spend 15% of their time on projects of their design – but it is quite the other to implement 'slack' at organizations where incentives and processes thwart such flexibility.

"There are flaws in our modern thinking about corporate innovation. For example, 'spread your bets, create many ideas', is flawed thinking, because an idea does not have any inherent value. Customers have multiple needs which are impossible for an organization to be aware of, and while many employees may have customer knowledge, companies rarely have a complete list of agreed upon customer needs. Is there anyone in your organization that knows all of the customer's needs? Is there an agreement across the organization on what the customer's needs are? Is there an agreement on whether the needs are unmet? If not, then how can there be an agreement on what products and services to produce?" – Tony Ulwick

That what works for one company will not necessarily work for another. Wolcott and Lippitz (2007) introduced a very useful model to segment the management side for your corporate innovation function. They use two axes to segment innovation management:

1. Resource authority – Is there a dedicated *pot of gold* allocated to corporate entrepreneurship, or are new business concepts funded in an ad hoc manner through divisional or corporate budgets or *slush funds*?
2. Organizational ownership – Who has primary responsibility within the organization for the creation of new businesses? In other words, who can start an innovation project? And why?

Based on these variables they have created four models of corporate entrepreneurship.

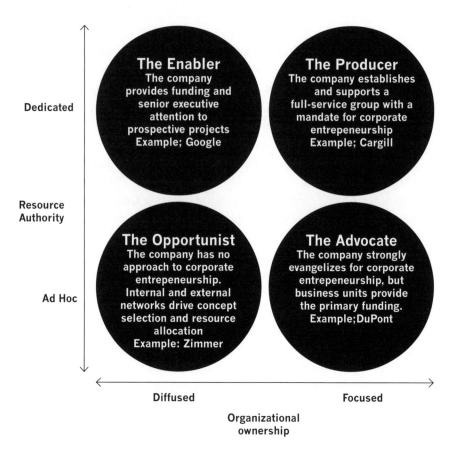

Figure 6.1 – Four models for corporate entrepreneurship

Four models of corporate entrepreneurship[26]

For more information on this topic, I am happy to refer to the article of Robert C. Wolcott and Michael J. Lippitz (2007) The Four Models of Corporate Entrepreneurship: https://sloanreview.mit.edu/article/the-four-models-of-corporateentrepreneurship

The producer model

There is a dedicated innovation department for breakthrough (Horizon 2/3) innovation with its own resources. The strategic goal is to exploit Future Growth opportunities. A good example here would be Cargill. In these organizations, there is a skilled team that can build new business and facilitate this process beyond the borders of the core business. Especially the latter makes it a different ball game. Leadership needs to be positioned strongly in the company and with enough internal decision authority. The challenges for this route exist in the integration path of successful projects into the core. Since the team's work is dedicated to new ventures, the need to link and connect with the mothership is less relevant. In that way, lack of business unit support can become an issue.

If a company seeks to conquer new growth domains and discover breakthrough opportunities, it should consider the producer model. Generally in practice, business units are not likely to pursue disruptive concepts and they often face strong near-term pressures that discourage investments in new growth platforms. The producer model helps overcome this and it can provide the necessary coordination for initiatives that involve complex technologies, or require the integration of certain capabilities across different business units.

Cargill

Cargill, the $75 billion global agriculture products and services company based in Wayzata, Minnesota, has established its Emerging Business Accelerator. As David Patchen, the group's founder and managing director, recalls, "Prior to the EBA, we lacked a clearly defined process for pursuing opportunities that fell outside the scope of existing business units and functions... We needed a new approach to complement our business units and Cargill Ventures [an internal venture group]."

Companies often don't know what to do with innovative concepts that don't fit an existing business, and financial incentives discourage the business leaders from absorbing near-term losses. That's where, for Cargill, the Emerging Business Accelerator comes in. The Accelerator aims to generate revenues from projects within three years so that it is not merely regarded as a source of funds for pie-in-the-sky research. It is important to emphasize the three years', because you need to have time to build a new business and show new growth numbers. We need to prove that money can be made at an early stage (data behind revenue streams), but real growth takes time.

The enabler model

When resource authority is high and organizational ownership diffuse, you work according to the *enabler* model. The goal here is to facilitate entrepreneurial employees and teams, meaning that there is serious funding for breakthrough innovations with senior attention. At Google for instance, breakthrough innovation is not the only goal, they also want to nourish their entrepreneurial culture. Independent funding and top executive attention is provided to future business leaders. There is structural flexibility for teams in these kinds of organizations to pursue projects. Due to the well-defined executive involvement, there needs to be a transparent innovation process with metrics and criteria for funding. Enabling teams to find and satisfy project champions and making sure that the enabler processes do not become a *black hole* for ideas can be a challenge.

Enabler programs can support efforts to enhance a company's culture. When an organization already enjoys strong collaboration and ideation, the enabler model can provide clear channels for concepts to be validated and funded. For companies seeking cultural transformation, enabler processes, in combination with new hiring criteria and staff development, can result in several employees becoming effective change agents. The enabler model is well-suited to environments in which concept development and experimentation can (already) be pursued economically throughout the organization.

Google's entrepreneurial culture, dynamic market and extraordinary access to capital, make the company difficult to replicate. Nonetheless, other organizations have had success using the enabler model. The Boeing Co. and Whirlpool Corp. have found out that dedicated funds for innovation combined with clear and disciplined processes for allocating those funds can go a long way toward unlocking latent entrepreneurial potential. Well-designed enabler practices also have the benefit of exposing senior management to ambitious, innovative young employees, allowing the company to identify and nurture future leaders.

The opportunist model

The opportunist model only works well in trusting corporate cultures that are open to experimentation and have diverse social networks behind the official hierarchy, in other words, places where multiple executives can say Yes. Without this type of environment, good ideas can easily fall through organizational cracks or receive insufficient funding. Consequently, the opportunist approach is not appropriate for many companies. When organizations get serious about organic growth, executives realize they need more than a diffused, ad hoc approach.

If organizations take innovation seriously, this model is not sufficient. When there is an *innovation function*, one person or a small team for example, the team is stretched over all categories. The team itself does not have money, so the business units need to finance this and, in that way, determine the scope of innovation. This means innovation is not that important, because the KPI setting in the business is not adjusted for real innovation, and it is narrowed down to *efficiency* innovations, which directly support the existing KPI set. Unfortunately, many companies follow this approach (unconsciously) when it comes to innovation.

The advocate model

What about cases in which funding isn't the issue? In the advocate model, a company assigns organizational ownership for the creation of new businesses and, at the same time, intentionally provides only modest budgets to the core group. Advocate organizations act as evangelists and innovation experts, facilitating corporate entrepreneurship in collaboration with business units. When the ownership is high, and resource authority is low, it means that corporate entrepreneurship is essential, but the business units need to fund it.

In my opinion, this is a suitable model for Renew the Core innovations, because with this type of innovation the core business resources are necessary. The weak side of this model, however, is that everything relies on the willingness of the business unit leader to innovate. To tackle this, the P&L responsible business unit leaders should have a set of relevant KPI's regarding innovation. If this is not the case, it is realistic to suppose that Optimize the Core innovations (efficiency) will dominate.

The advocate model strategic goal is to reinvigorate or transform business units and support corporate entrepreneurship teams, and companies that want to accelerate the growth of established divisions. The limited resources, which this model requires, make it possible that managers tailor their initiatives to the interests of existing lines of business, and employees have to collaborate intensively throughout the organization. This enhances the potential fit of opportunities to a company's operations, but also requires leadership to ensure that projects do not become too incremental. Advocates exist to help business units do what they can't accomplish on their own, but must accomplish to remain vital and relevant.

In large corporations, multiple models can be supported concurrently at different levels and functions. IBM, for instance, maintains a hybrid producer-advocate team — the (famous) Emerging Business Opportunities program — that has generated over $15 billion of new revenues as of 2005. Meanwhile, IBM's Think-place and Innovation Jams encourage ideation and networking in the fashion of an advocate model. Like an enabler, IBM also supports divisional processes for corporate entrepreneurship, some of which transfer projects to the Emerging Business Opportunities program for development and scaling.

 See the checklist: Determine the organization of your corporate entrepreneurship function.

6.3   Two sets of rules and policies

 See the checklist: Say yes, to innovation rules and policies.

An existing organization has policies to protect the established business from risk, reputation damage, hiring the wrong people or not buying IT that is security-proof. Policies and processes are developed for *continuity*, so the big organization can execute. When the CEO decides to work on innovative projects with ninja teams in a Lean Startup way, the policies and processes that are at play will not facilitate fast learning. Most impediments are on a tactical level. For example, HR prescribes that you can only hire people with a certain seniority level, or IT forces innovation teams to use existing IT platforms and doesn't have time for custom jobs because innovation teams are not part of their priorities. Another familiar problem is that Finance asks for the return on investment of a startup.

Some facts about (most) established organizations: [27]
- Established organizations are designed to execute on a repeatable and scalable business model.
- Innovation teams are temporary teams, designed to search for a repeatable and scalable business model.
- Most of the time established organizations have resources, distribution channels, Sales teams and money, all designed to execute on the existing business, not to facilitate the search of a new business model.
- Resources for the execution are, paradoxically, an obstacle for the processes of search for a new business model.
- Established organizations need new and different processes for innovation, while the existing processes for execution remain.
- In this way, the resources of an established organization can also be used to facilitate the innovation processes.

Imagine that your startup team is going fast, learning relentlessly fast, validating problems, identifying customer persona's and launching prototypes in the market. The team is on fire! They want to start selling a product that does not yet exist on a fake door web shop. Now it is getting complicated. IT does not allow the team to build a web shop in a non-corporate 'Saas' solution. Legal says you open the door to lawsuits from customers, because you are fooling them. All remarks are legit, but does it facilitate fast learning? No. So how to turn this around?

The idea is to create (bottom-up) a second set of rules and a process that facilitates the creation of these new rules. These teams should start working in a new way to understand how Lean Startup works within the unique context of a specific organization. But also, to avoid highly theoretical 'what if...' discussions with staff departments about the rules that might block innovation or not.

Within a big global fast moving consumer goods company I helped teams create these kinds of custom-made policies and rules. I agreed, in this case, with the highest internal sponsor that he would function as an escalation path, when we cannot move the needle internally when we need to get a 'yes' for a new custom-made rule. (At that time, the term venture board did not exist yet, but today this would be a function of the venture board). The process was that when the staff department got a request from an innovation team, they had two days to ponder upon the request, in which the default answer was 'yes'. When, for some reason, the answer was 'no', they had to explain their reasons to the senior internal sponsor, upon which (explanation) the final decision was made. Before we actually started with this process, we had already identified people from staff departments within the organization who we knew were innovative. We trained them in how the corporate startup teams work, so they would experience the power of the methodologies and tools, but also experience the difference in the way an established organization operates.

At the end of the training, we asked the participants to think proactively with the innovation teams, when they came with an alternative rule that would facilitate innovation. The innovation teams started to fill in the form Say yes to innovation rules and policies [28] and would send it to the specific department/contact person. Then the previous formulated process would start. The new rules were of course codified and shared with the organization, so new innovation teams could benefit from the pioneering work of the staff departments in collaboration with the innovation teams.

6.4   Managing the startup to scale-up process

"Because entrepreneurship is always about institution-building, it is, necessarily, about management" – Eric Ries

The idea of building the business model innovation capability, is becoming more evident in the life of ever decreasing life cycles. Shrinking lifetimes of established business models are tied to the fact that the benefits of (digitally) transforming those business models are increasingly questioned.

That said, Clayton Christensen et al. proposed: "To achieve successful business model innovation, focus on creating new business models, rather than changing existing ones. As business model interdependencies arise, the ability to create new businesses within existing business units is lost. The resources and processes that work so perfectly in their original business model do so because they have been honed and optimized for delivering on the priorities of that model."

To give an example, my team coached a corporate startup, because a specific product had suffered a decline in sales and had a problem in its retention. Through interviewing and observing the customers in their surroundings, we learned about the *job to be done* for the customer and the difficulties they faced trying to do this job. The solution was that we created a different business model with a couple of different angles:
- We created an acquisition strategy that builds quality leads for sales.
- We created a subscription model on the product, including a platform with relevant content for the customer group, and helped them to sort out a couple of difficulties.

The profit formula became different as well. The costs went down in the sales force but went up in the online content platform and the maintenance of it. This had to be organized because the existing business unit did not have these skills. Besides that, the Sales people needed to be trained in a new way of making sales. The product was already sold online: so there was no need for the Sales to do *hard* sell. It was more an evaluation of how the product was performing and finding out new opportunities for multiple up-sells.

Renewing the Core business, as described in the case above, is a management challenge. There is no one size fits all. So how can your company increase the odds of winning in Renewing the Core business?

Let's have a look at some examples for Renew the Core innovations. First of all, to build a new business must be a deliberate strategic choice. It was to the advantage of Ball Corporation that they entered the aerospace sector and leveraged their expertise in the interface of metal and glass. Fujitsu gained an edge by entering healthcare that was based on its ability to leverage its expertise in surface chemistry. Consequently, the idea is to use the assets and capabilities that are already present as a competitive advantage.

The challenge, on the other hand, lies in the resource allocation process. From a financial or risk management perspective, jumping from metal and glass into the aerospace sector does not make sense. Is the company willing to put its resources into these kinds of strategic jumps? That's why Renew the Core innovations should always be a deliberate choice made by the executive board and should be a part (as a set of KPI's) of the P&L of the business. It is the transition path to harnessing the existing business without fear of disruption.

However, if the innovation strategy does not have back-up from the board, it will not get the attention that it needs to succeed. A necessary step is to incorporate the innovation the strategy in the corporate strategy.

6.5   Pathways to business model discovery and validation

In the 10x Growth Machine Framework, the innovation process is a process of ideation, validation and scale. (In Chapter 4 we described the methodology in much more detail.) Depending on which playing field the innovation takes place, the integration and scaling-up trajectory will be different challenges. From the point of view of managerial strategy, the most challenging trajectory is innovation in the Renew the Core playing field, for different reasons:

1. Internal tensions: Renewing the existing business model, for example going digital, impacts the existing business. Why would people collaborate on initiatives that undermine their own position?
2. Using core company assets: To renew the existing business requires collaboration with the same existing business. When the startup team has a recurring revenue model, the business needs to be integrated in a new or existing business unit. In the path to get to this

a repeatable revenue model, the team needs access to the existing distribution channels or access to R&D people. This comes on top of the current priorities of the business. Furthermore, we want to avoid a *not invented here* reflex. This means that scaling-up the integration trajectory needs to be approached as a deliberate change management process.

Optimizing the Core should be a managerial job of the core business itself. Isn't continuous improvement of the existing business the job of *good management*?

Let's avoid ill-positioned innovation labs becoming a pipeline for the business because of their Optimize the Core innovations. Creating the future is about building new business, completely separate with an own P&L. Then the real question becomes: What to separate and what to integrate?

As a general guiding principle in the discovery and validation phase, the advice of Marcel Bogers et al., is not to settle too quickly on the organizational structure of emerging business models. They write: "The lesson for any organization wanting to explore new business models, is not to settle too quickly on a structure for the new business. The organizational structure can more usefully be thought of as one of the essential building blocks of the business model – that is, as an aspect of the new business that needs to be fully explored and experimented with before you can learn what works best.

The Business Model Canvas framework developed by Alexander Osterwalder and Yves Pigneur has become a very popular way to understand the potential building blocks of business models. [...] However, organizational designs and the associated organizational tensions that emerge during the process of business model exploration, are not well addressed by the existing tools. Companies exploring new business models may not fully recognize that these tensions will almost inevitably emerge, and thus may be ill-prepared to manage them. Understanding these tensions should help in managing the challenges of concurrent business models."

The tensions between new and established business arise from the following disparities[29]:
- Disrupting the existing business model.
- Cannibalizing the existing customer base.
- Destroying or undermining the value of the existing distribution network.
- Compromising the quality of service offered to customers.
- Undermining the company's reputation and brand power.
- Destroying the capabilities (processes, skills etc.) the companies had built.
- Shifting customers from high-value activities to low-margin ones.

According to Ralph-Christian Ohr, the bigger the conflicts between the two business models, the lower the possibility that the two models can share any synergies among them, and the more appropriate a separation strategy becomes.

A key question, involved in business model innovation, is then: What is the adequate organizational setting to discover, validate and scale new business models concurrently to running existing (and often still successful) ones? Are they to be separated as dedicated units, even spun out, to unfold and gain traction? Or is integration with selected units of the core business the best precondition for emerging business models to thrive in a corporate environment?

Based on Tushman and O'Reilly (2016), an ambidextrous approach (which means we separate the business, but not in the sense that we cannot use the assets of the mother company anymore) is deployed if a venture is of high strategic relevance, and its synergies with core business are high, suggesting a substantial leverage of core assets and capabilities, as well as an ultimate integration into core business in the course of scaling. Under certain circumstances, the most appropriate strategy is to either separate or integrate the new way of competing, but not right from the start. As Ohr describes the conflict when the new business model serves a market in a way that is strategically similar to the existing business, but the two ways of competing is a cause of conflict, the firm faces a difficult challenge. On the one hand, it stands to benefit through integration of the two, and exploits the synergies between them, but on the other hand, integration might lead to serious internal problems because of the conflicts (cannibalization etc.). In this situation, it might be better to separate for some time and then slowly merge the two concepts, to minimize the disruption from the conflicts.

The main challenge a company is facing when it chooses this phased integration strategy, is keeping the new unit sufficiently autonomous, as well as preparing it for the eventual incorporation. This is an ultimate test of managing stakeholders, managing internal dynamics and moving forward at the same time.

Competing with core business resources

One of my customers started executing accelerators in a more systematically way. New teams entered each quarter, and those that were more mature needed some initial help from the supply chain. It started with a couple of hours per week. To arrange this, the high-placed sponsor of the startup team made some personal calls. How to manage the extra work became the problem of the manager of the supply chain and, a couple of weeks later, the team needed two days per week. Suddenly, managerial decisions had to be made on allocating resources for this project. So it turns out, in a case like this, a personal phone call does not work.

Let's have a look at the next model, *organizing internal ventures*. The independent business unit can be built from scratch. In this scenario, the *strategic relevance* is high, but operationally the capabilities of the mothership are not needed. Netflix/Qwikster is a good example. Qwikster was the offline DVD renting service. You ordered your movie online and it was sent by mail. Netflix is the online subscription model for content and original series. The metrics that were measured in the business model and the capabilities that were needed were different to the Qwikster business. In this case, an independent business unit is the way to move forward.

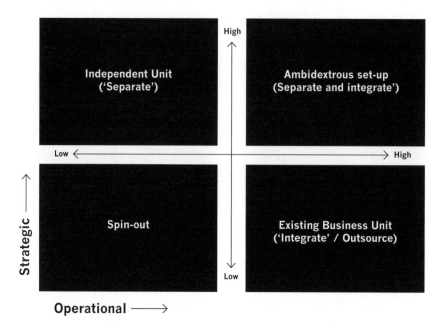

Figure 6.2 – Organizing internal ventures, Ohr 2017

If you look at the spin-out scenario, Ciba vision is an example. They make contact lenses, but also developed a drug that combated a debilitating eye disease. The product had various sales channels, different technologies and different manufacturing process. The strategic relevance for the core business was low and the drug (to cure the eye disease) did not need capabilities from the core business, contact lens manufacturers. The spin-out scenario is most relevant.

The existing business unit scenario can be explained with Apple. Apple designs the iPhone, but outsources the production of the iPhone to Foxconn in China. Apple can build the capabilities themselves, though from an economic perspective, that does not make sense.

In the case of strategically important business model innovation, we can conclude that a separated setting, it turns out, is indicated for discovering and validating business models, involving more or less linkage with the core business units.

The golden rule is not to bring the new business back into the core business too early. The chances of its suffocation under the weight of the core business are huge. When should it be brought back? The business model is completely validated on the right and left side of the Business Model Canvas. But more importantly, there is a repeatable sales map (monthly recurring revenue model), and indicators for Future Growth are validated. This means that:

1. We bring (with the business) a repeatable revenue stream with a healthy business model.
2. We know how we can grow it faster, using the assets of the core company.

In other words, if we have a complete sales map with growth targets in place, it becomes a matter of perfecting execution.

Markides and Charitou concluded that several variables can influence how well a new business model is managed. For example, companies that adopt a separation strategy will do better if they give operational and financial autonomy to their units, but still maintain a close watch over the strategy of the unit. They should encourage cooperation between the unit and the parent, through common incentive and reward systems, allowing the units to develop their own cultures and budgetary systems, where each unit has its CEO, which is transferred internally from the organization (rather than hiring an outsider). Similarly, companies that adopt an integration strategy will do better if they designate a top management sponsor in the organization, who has the power to protect the new business from interference by the parent. The new business model should be treated as a wonderful new opportunity to grow the business (rather than as a threat) and the strengths of the traditional business should be leveraged to find ways to differentiate, rather than imitate, the strategies of their attackers. This task should be approached in a proactive, strategic manner, rather than as a hasty knee-jerk reaction to a problem, and the extreme care should be taken not to suffocate the new business with the existing policies of the firm.

Managing the internal tensions, emotions and distrust is a crucial capability for scaling-up in the playing field of Renew the Core. This is the playing field in which an integration/separation strategy needs to be implemented, step-by-step: the same goes for the use of capabilities of the core business.

For the innovation to be able to scale and become part of the standing organization, it requires an expanding group of people to work towards the same goal and with the same mindset. The entrepreneurial mindset from different to the *business-as usual* mindset, in the sense that it requires a pro-active way of determining what will and needs to happen, rather than a *rule-following* mentality.

As the innovation scales, more business functions will be exposed to it and supporting functions will also need to understand the innovation, its business model and growth targets. They should understand how they, from their professional expertise, could help in achieving its growth targets even if this contradicts their performance targets. The permission and mandate to follow this way of working and embracing the entrepreneurial mindset should come from senior management, represented by the venture board. To make the collaboration work, transparency on goals, tensions, progress and vision, and communicating regularly between the founder, the team, the venture board sponsor of the project and the relevant business owners is crucial. Venture board meetings should happen regularly and the venture team should show the progress on clear KPI's and discuss openly the tensions that arise while scaling-up.

Points to ponder

It's mandatory to achieve CEO commitment and alignment among executive management, before putting systematic effort into truly explorative activities. Otherwise, exploration oriented innovation will eventually be doomed, resources – wasted, and people – frustrated. Every corporate organization or government agency is dealing with disruption. Most of them have concluded that *business as usual* can't go on.

Innovation isn't a single activity; it is a process from start to deployment. In *exploitation or execution* engines, committees and broad stakeholder involvement make sense, because experience, knowledge and data from the past allow better decision-making. Though in *innovation engines* there isn't enough data to decide between competing ideas/projects (since nobody's been in the future), so the teams need to gather facts outside their building quickly.

An automatic, data-driven, Lean innovation process will deliver continuous innovation and disruptive breakthroughs with speed and urgency. However, one of the key topics within corporate innovation is how to measure, track and fund the different corporate startups. That is the topic of the next chapter.

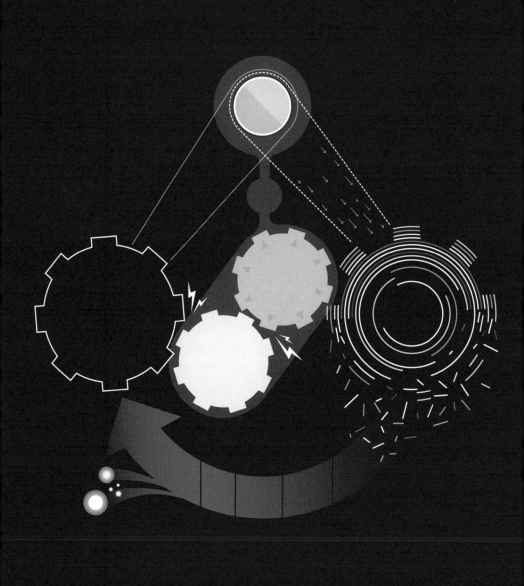

Chapter 7
Transformation for growth

– FROM MINIMAL VIABLE INNOVATION PROJECTS TO SYSTEMATIC GROWTH MACHINE

Transformation is a word that is used a lot without an attempt to define what it means. What do we need to transform and why? In this chapter, I present a change management approach in going from the minimal viable Growth Machine to an entrepreneurial system that co-exists with the big organization.

To build the Growth Machine, the growth transformation canvas provides senior executives with the structure of building blocks that need to be implemented if future growth is the goal.

From my experience in working with corporate startups, I noticed that (from a change management perspective) a certain logic and chronology can be applied to become successful. In this chapter, we will elaborate on the change management pathways that serve as guidelines to navigate through the, sometimes, harsh realities of corporate life.

"You've got to be flexible and take some risks. Some things work, and some don't. Corporate entrepreneurship is fundamentally a learning process."
– Mike Giersch, Vice President for strategy at IBM

7.1   Phase one: Art of the Start – build first success, learn how it works and create allies

"In the initial stages you need to have a C-level champion to bring it further. Our CEO and President consumer Dairy gave me support. I had a good back-up. But prove your word, build success and stay under the radar in the beginning." – Aniruddha Kusurkar, Global Commercial Director at FrieslandCampina

For companies that are about to embark on a new program of corporate entrepreneurship, the following high-level summary of tips should provide some guidance:

1. The Art of the Start

If you have an idea about where your company can grow and win, you have the moral obligation to start. Gather three ideas, train some early innovators in your company and start ideating, validate and scale new propositions. Find your team, your senior sponsor to provide some good back-up and start learning. Start learning how this new way of working is thriving in your own unique company. Every corporate organization is different. Different people, processes, culture. What we often see is that it is already difficult to start. The reason for this is that the core business is used to analyzing every step to avoid risks. That is the same reason why starting something different is, precisely what it is, *different*. One of the values of the core business is to reduce variance/difference. There is an inherent tension between what the innovator wants to achieve and what the mission of the core business actually is. You cannot solve this upfront. To change effectively, instead of the traditional approach where management is responsible for thinking and the workforce for the labor, thinking and doing needs to happen at the same time.

2. Don't create blueprints, develop a growth mindset

We can create blueprints on how the perfect organization should work. We can hire expert consultants that do restructuring programs. The problem is, these don't solve your growth problem. We also build frameworks and tools, but we don't tell you that if you follow these rigidly the pot of gold will be found on the other side of the rainbow. There are no four steps to success or magic formulas. We need to be realistic and share with you a sensible approach. We are not in the business of selling illusions. Building new growth models and implementing the system is tough. It challenges your comfort zones and those of the organization. You will work against deep ingrained patterns of thinking, being and doing. Leadership, leading yourself so you can lead others, is a crucial element that should be based on a new set of habits. Some call this the growth mindset, working on opportunities and slaying corporate obstacles.

3. Executive sponsorship

In my experience you need executive sponsorship for:

1. *The strategic vision.* For growth, this needs to be consistent with the capabilities that corporate entrepreneurship can leverage. Too narrow and a company will get more of the same, too broad and people won't know where to start. When everyone knows what they're looking for, they're more likely to find it.
2. *Delineate objectives and get permissions and boundaries clear.* Start with a small team, clearly define and communicate the company's objectives for corporate entrepreneurship. Is the aim to build radical new growth platforms or to renovate existing business units? Is cultural transformation part of the equation, or is the goal to unleash latent entrepreneurial talent? What are the boundaries in which we can innovate?

This is especially true when your growth opportunities lie in the playing fields Renew the Core and Future Growth. These opportunities can create conflicts among the lines of existing businesses. Furthermore, when we want to work differently (moving forward), it can only happen if the leadership stands behind this idea. At the end of the day, when it comes to change, people in the organization will look up to the leadership to see if it this idea is embraced by the executives. Any kind of change leads to uncertainty and to reduce uncertainty, people need confirmation from the leading managers of the organization. Clarity and clearly signed internal communications are crucial.

Seven-step plan for C-level alignment and growth strategy

Creating growth strategies is one thing. To implement them is the real challenge. Alignment and clear understanding on where new growth can happen, is organized through dialogue sessions with the executive board. For execution, follow these important steps and plant it right:

1. Disruptive analysis: What kind of new business models in the periphery of the market do we see? What kinds of VC investments are made in which domains? Are there any technological developments? Is consumer behavior changing? We cover all the early warning signs mentioned before. We will look no further than five years. In practice, it is already challenging to let people think further than three years. Imagination can be difficult in a corporate environment.

2. Current business model: Can we sketch our current business model? You will see that different executives can vary on who the customer is, what the value proposition is. This is not bad, but it is good to make the differences explicit and create a shared understanding of the current business.

3. Strengths/Weaknesses: Where is our current business vulnerable? What assets do we have now, that gives us a competitive advantage over the competition? What is our competitive advantage over the competition? Based on insights from the disruptive analysis, we create *points of view* on where the money is to be made in the future. We can call this an innovation thesis/vision.

4. Growth opportunity areas: From this point of view, we create *growth opportunity areas*. These are overall buckets that define *new growth* and provide a focus on *where to play*.

5. Deep diving in the market: with the growth opportunities we deep dive into the market to understand what kind of *jobs to be done* are not solved well enough or not solved at all. What kind of acquisition targets can we define? What is the size of the opportunity? Build some new prototype solutions that solve the problem and map out these solutions on the three playing fields, i.e. Optimize the Core, Renew the Core and Future Growth.
6. Allocate resources: When the portfolio is in place and is aligned with the board (based on the three playing fields), it is time to allocate resources and start the validation process.
7. Venture boards: train the executive board and relevant stakeholders in the content of the innovation portfolio and how to act as an internal investor.

4. Determine the corporate entrepreneurship model

Companies need to select the right model (enabler, advocate or producer), develop a team with the required capabilities and provide the necessary resources. Think big but start small. This is the minimal viable version of your Growth Machine.

5. Create ambassadors and neutralize the naysayers

Working on new growth opportunities and implementing methodologies (like Lean Startup) to learn and validate fast, attract other early adopters in the company. These are the people that always have been a little bit different. They are innovators at heart. They look actively at how to innovate in the organization and make it work better. These are the people with the crazy ideas (from the perspective of the status quo), but also those that were probably disappointed a couple of times in their change endeavors. You should build corporate and divisional leadership consensus through extensive communication. Understand the motivations of vested interests and determine how to collaborate with or mitigate the opposition.

6. Quick wins, speed of learning and kill-rates

Corporate entrepreneurship is new for most companies. That's why it is important to build credibility with tangible performance and to learn lessons to protect programs from marginalization or cancellation. One of the key elements at the beginning of this journey is to build success and tangible results and then create a movement, bottom-up. Increase the speed of learning 10x, share this in the organization and kill projects faster (also the pet or zombie projects in your organization). A key element is also to find ambassadors within staff departments like HR and IT. These people can enable you on a tactical level to execute on fast learning and experimentation.

Interview with Stijn Dietz, COO from Unit4, an international producer and supplier of company software and related services.

Why did Unit4 start an accelerator program? What were the envisioned strategic goals?

Our portfolio of small, local and mature software businesses needed innovation to remain meaningful and competitive. However, given single-digit growth and the role of this portfolio as cash cow, there was little appetite for spending much on large innovation projects. We wanted to embrace the Lean Startup way of doing innovation, where our people would learn to "think big, start small and fail fast". This brings us to another objective of the accelerator program, learning and training our people, especially our biggest talents, for talent retention purposes. So basically, we wanted innovation, as well as learning, to be innovative with limited budgets. We knew this would introduce a positive vibe, which would trigger other great things in the company.

How has this program, until now, been adopted by the company? What is going well? What needs improvement?

So far it has brought us what we wanted: actual innovation, knowledge for the participants and stakeholders, and a positive vibe across the company because of it. To trigger this, we have been very active with internal communication during the program, though we have now reached a point where it is important to keep the momentum and bring the innovations to scale (business model validation). This is something that is not easy without the structure of an accelerator program.

Can you describe the (governance) model around the accelerator? How do you allocate resources (time/money)? Is it a normal stage-gate process or is it something different?

We are still relatively early in the process. Our current set-up is that we have re-allocated five existing resources from different functions (Product, Software Development, Marketing, Sales, Customer Success) to become our dedicated innovation team. It owns the portfolio of early innovations to bring them to scale, and secondly, are the champions in further extending the reach of the Lean Startup methodology. This team does not do everything on their own, they leverage other people part-time when, for instance, something needs to be built or operationally implemented.

Every month there is a venture board with four people from our leadership team: CEO, Chief Product, Chief Commercial and Chief Technology. The venture board decides on resourcing, funding and continuation based on pre-defined measures of success.

How do you scale a successful project within Unit4? Which criteria do you use? Would you use the same approach for your accelerator projects?

The most important criteria to scale are early proof points for future commercial success, which can be a combination of any relevant leading indicators that (when extrapolated) would imply that we solve a problem for many customers at healthy margins. Another thing is that the innovation is fully in line with our overarching purpose, strategy and value proposition towards the customer.

What are the next steps for Unit 4 when it comes to their innovation ambitions?

Making the Dual Core operating model work. We are dedicated to build a Growth Machine next to our execution engine. We are in the early stages of our journey; we have just assigned innovation capacity and have not brought an innovation to scale yet.

What would you recommend to those readers who want to start an innovation program like this?

My biggest recommendation is to try and start it. At the very least, a group of talented employees will have had a great time and learned a new skill set that is very relevant in these times. But I'm sure some viable innovations will come out of it as well.
A critical aspect of such programs is the leadership support and, preferably, the CEO as a sponsor and/or champion. This makes it much easier to keep the momentum after the accelerator is done and you are back on your own. Not all leaders are comfortable with the Lean Startup approach and innovation accounting, and you don't want to prematurely kill very promising business models.

7.2 Phase two: Governance – implement system building blocks, engage the organization

Communicate success, executive focus and define business metrics that matter

First, teams have run their ideas in a Lean Startup way. They have prob-ably presented their findings on a Demo Day, so people see that this way of working brings results and inspires people differently. The first ques-tions arise: How can we scale this way of working? How can we attract the talent that we need for building a new business? How do we retain them? What about IT? Legal? Can we sell products that we don't have?

Now is the time for the executive board to be clear in their communication on the fact that the company is moving towards the future and is driving next to the current business. This is the second operating system (the 10x Growth Machine) of a new business. Next, define the key business metrics that the board is overlooking. It is good to mention that it is a new way of working, that this is a time in which we need to reflect on our current ways of working and how we can design a second set of processes and rules that facilitates the fast learning of the Growth Machine. Don't be vague; communicate with the organization and share success. Start build-ing symbols that start to represent new ways of thinking and working. In FrieslandCampina they brand their innovation program Milkubator and give it its own look and feel.

Create scarcity
This might be counterintuitive, but as always, don't scale too fast if you don't understand the mechanisms on a smaller level. I don't believe in big transformation programs. Statistics show that many change programs fail, supporting my point of view. Though many companies still follow the top-down-blueprint approach and think that implementation is a linear process. As I have mentioned before, understanding the emotional dynam-ics in an organization and then effectively intervening are crucial factors. Numbers and logic alone don't beat human emotions.

Moreover, what we see in successful innovation programs is that they start small, but are also strict in selecting the individuals that can enter such programs. More and more corporates understand that entrepreneurship is a very different way of operating and should be incentivized differently. Entrepreneurship is passion-driven and without passion you will not overcome many of the (big and small) bumps in the road. It is a risky endeavor and the upside should be greater than a base salary. Intrapreneurs should feel the pains and gains real startups have. Bootstrap the resources and make it as real as possible. Scarcity is about selecting the individuals that can fulfill this role and are passion-driven. But it is also about creating the scarcity mindset. Excess of resources kills creativity and the entrepreneurial way of working.

First identify champions on all levels

It's time to identify people that can become champions of the new way of working. After C-level, it is essential to organize the same dialogue sessions with the levels below. When the *growth opportunity areas* are defined, the question becomes: How to source and judge these initiatives. It is time to involve the organization and get the business unit directors onboard. They run the P&L and are in charge of the resource allocation process. This means that if they do not embrace the innovation ambitions and understand that this requires a different way of working and resources, your innovation activities will become a theatrical play. This process always starts with people that do *get it*. There are still early adopters, but also laggards; and the latter can have good arguments to back up their skepticism. You don't change this by facing it head-on. Show results that help them. To build initial success, we focus on driving the core innovations with more speed and accuracy. If we can fix a broken product in the core business, we directly help the P&L directors. Effective change starts if you help people in the right positions do their work better.

Involve staff: build a playbook of different rules and policies

The entrepreneurial way of working is about fast learning, instead of going through long product cycles and internal debates. We launch minimal viable products in the market, which means that we create web shops and start selling a product that does not yet exist. You can imagine that colleagues from the Legal department will not automatically appreciate this; from their perspective, we have just created a way for customers to sue the company. Or what about sharing IP in this way? What do we do with the mail addresses we collect? We also want to build fast platforms online to test some assumptions around brands and buying behavior. IT can ask critical questions around privacy and data protection. The trap is that we start arguing and accuse the other party of being old-fashioned, bureaucratic and vice versa. Both are right. They have a valid point from the execution perspective; they want to protect the mothership, which is their role. If we blame each other for performing our role, we don't create understanding. We need to ask them for advice. They are intelligent people and understand that the world is changing. The question should be: How can we enable fast learning, so that we can build new revenue growth, but also protect the mothership from harm? Then, let's create a bottom-up process in which we identify rules and policies from the mothership that blocks the entrepreneurial way of working. Can we develop a second set of rules, policies and processes that helps the Growth Machine further?

Act as an investor, identify portfolio gaps

To understand if we hit the growth curve, it is important to shift from the execution paradigm and established accounting metrics to the venture capital mindset and relevant metrics. As mentioned previously, one of the challenges is *the curse of big thinking*. The common way to get resources would be to make the business case big upfront. This is a precarious way to move forward with big projects because it creates a dynamic in which failing is not an option. How can we switch the mindset of executives to think, see and act as an internal investor to our corporate startup teams? Do the teams show progress on relevant impact metrics? Did they validate the problem in the market on a bigger scale? The challenge is not the theory, the challenge is building a portfolio of experiments, tapping into new opportunities with high speed, spreading risks around the three playing fields (Optimize the Core, Renew the Core, Future Growth), put your money where your mouth is and build new business.

Tip: View the tool of the metric board and read paragraph 3.4 on metered funding

After doing this for a couple of months, the speed of learning goes up, the kill rates of projects go up and portfolio gaps are getting more visible. When corporate startups are successful and need investment money to scale, you start competing with projects and the resource allocation process from the core business. To give a simple example, when we coach teams in, for example, the FMCG market, at some point we reach success and need help from the supply chain. This starts with a couple of hours per month. Gradually it becomes more serious than that. Were we clear upfront about the resources we needed, to become successful at a later stage? Because an investor board is a decision-making process, the key to make successful decisions, is to prepare these meetings carefully and execute proper stakeholder management before the meeting takes place.

When working with accelerators or other types of high intensity programs, you will identify the entrepreneurial talent in your organization. But how do you nurture and develop this? How do you incentivize your intrapreneurial talent? Can entrepreneurship be a career path within our company?

7.3   Phase three: Scale – perfect the practice, build A-teams within the organization

Perfecting the daily practice

When first success is achieved, and investor board meetings have found a rhythm, it is time to evaluate how entrepreneurial management is operating in the corporate context. Like the minimal viable product concept has the goal to learn how a product or services works on a small scale, in this context it means that we understand how the minimal viable Growth Machine works in your company. When we understand this, scaling of activities is allowed, if the ambition is to build a Growth Machine that systematically churns out new business models. The most important thing to start implementing, is the new processes that drive an innovative way of working. In the daily practicalities, change needs to be implemented. Take meetings for example, most of the time highly ineffective. Remind each other to keep it simple, the facts are outside the building. Challenge each other on how to test a certain idea instead of trying to reach consensus around what might or might not work. Here is where your ambassadors can play an important role and this is the challenge for investor boards too. They need to make decisions, not share opinions based on previous experience. Sometimes corporate clients ask us if we can add a famous entrepreneur to their investor boards. Though it might be appealing, famous entrepreneurs will always share their experiences based on the past. We want to implement a scientific and data-driven approach, in which the market shows us where we need to invest. It is the *Moneyball* analogy.

Hire the best and build great teams

This can make or break your innovation adventure. You need people that can solve real problems and push it from idea to product, using their own observations and experience to push for constant incremental improvements. Without this kind of talent, you will not create a high-performance Growth Machine. The best people will prove their worth and earn their cost. Another important thing about hiring the best people, besides an outstanding knowledge of content, they should be team players. At Startupbootcamp we observed on a big scale that team fit is crucial. If teams cannot collaborate, the Growth Machine will not produce new revenue models and it will not be the first time that a (corporate) startup fails because of bad team dynamics. You could write a book on this topic alone, but to keep it simple we use psychological profiling to build complementary teams, to craft the teams and select the right people. To accomplish this, we follow a straightforward three-step process:

1. Individual interview with four/five different people.
2. Understand your psychological profile, especially how you perform under pressure and in mixed groups of people.
3. We give a test case to understand your problem-solving skills.

Hire slow, but fire fast. Corporate startup teams are too small to postpone tough decisions, it will immediately influence the performance of the team. Besides profiling the teams, as previously mentioned, it is also about managing the tensions and talking about topics that matter instead of avoiding conflict. With pre-mediation we try to manage this process the best we can. This means we have a team check-up regularly to understand if there are certain unspoken tensions in the team. Don't underestimate this part.

Foster ownership in the line organization

During the scaling-up phase of implementing this way of working, innovations might increase in value and impact, but costs and resource demands are also higher. Sceptics might say that the costs are disproportionately high in relation to the value delivery. There is a serious chance that the line organization will not quickly experience the benefits of the innovations, especially since initially the goals or targets of the line organization do not include the growth of innovation. The reality is that middle management will view all these innovations as blocking their own way of working. It is imperative that, when resources are required from the core business, the ownership of the innovations is transferred to the line organization with its appointed business owner as quickly as possible. That means that they will decide upon the fate of the innovation. Working on achieving real mental ownership of the business owner and its innovation, is key to success. Goals of the innovation should be aligned with the growth (strategic) goals of the organization.

"Successful innovation is a feat, not of intellect but of will. Its difficulty consists in the resistance and uncertainties incident to doing what has not been done before." – Joseph Schumpeter

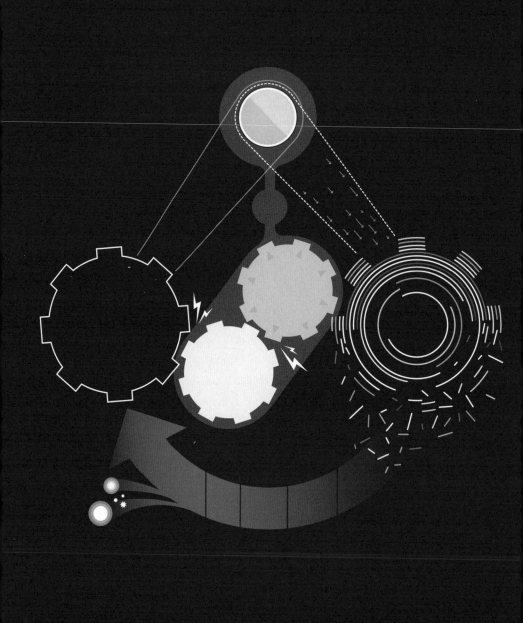

Afterword
Envisioning a Future-Proof organization

Innovation is a challenging journey and there is no one size fits all. Every company is unique, the people, the culture and its history. According to leading market research firms, about 75% of consumer-packaged goods and retail products fail to earn even $7.5 million during their first year[30]. According to Harvard Business School, each year more than 30,000 new consumer products are launched and 80% of them fail.

We started the journey to identify the *growth dilemma* corporates are facing, stating that new economic growth comes from Renew the Core and Future Growth types of innovation. What's wrong with the corporate system however, is that the way it measures success causes an over-investment in efficiency innovations and makes it very hard to invest in market creating innovation (disruptive). Kraft Heinz is an example of over-investing in efficiency innovation with the result that growth numbers are plummeting. Growth is crucial not only for the company but also for people and society. If you are not growing, then there is no future for the people who are giving their lives for the enterprise. We come to the conclusion that:

1. Long-term growth from non-incremental innovations should be a top priority to enable corporations to survive into the future.
2. The way the corporate is structured to make money, is blocking this very crucial element for future growth.

The need to setup a different system to create growth from non-incremental innovations becomes a must, and top priority of CEO's. As the KPMG study shows[31] conventional wisdom is telling us to invest 10% in Future

Growth innovation, but nowadays these numbers are doubled. Change will happen, the only question is when it will strike your company. Most of the innovation budget is still going to R&D, which is a great way to improve the products, but it does not tell us how to win in the market. To create an understanding of how to win in the market, we need to develop entre-preneurial capabilities to launch product prototypes and new business models. We need to focus on growth areas and start developing a portfolio of multiple bets in the market. With the entrepreneurial mindset, a clear end-to-end innovation process with phases and milestones, the corporate venture team needs to start validation in the market. When success could be on the horizon, the venture board, venture team and relevant business owners should meet in a regular cadence to talk about progress, invest-ments and upcoming tensions between the venture team and the busi-ness. This means transforming the board of companies into acting like an internal investor and mentor of the team.

The organization that is Future-Proof is able to build the Growth Machine (dual operating system) with a venture capital perspective on investments, people with an entrepreneurial mindset and the right processes, metrics and growth targets to make it work. The transformation effort is big, and the upside when successful, is immeasurable.

Transformation journey to excellence

Basically, what it comes down to is learning a new way of thinking and implementing this in daily practice, enforced by the right processes and KPI's. Learning is difficult. We ask board members to act as internal in-vestors and be relentless truth seekers when teams present data. Asking good questions is the master tool, giving opinions is irrelevant. At the same time, they need to provide permission for the teams to really work differently and protect them from the organization. The whole paradigm of failure is replaced by fast learning. Rewarding learning ability is cru-cial. Besides showing new behavior, leaders would feel comfortable with ambiguity and uncertainty. Placing multiple bets, through portfolio man-agement, investing more money when the data looks good but the numbers are still small, requires a strong sense of urgency and guts, to push through this way to new growth.

How effective you are in innovation comes down to how competent the organization is. As ancient Chinese wisdom tells us: talk does not cook rice. It requires leadership and this cannot be taught, it depends on who you are and the quality of the questions that you ask. Leadership is not determined by a position, but measurable by the consequences of what you do. The organization that you have is a reflection of the leadership style and quality deployed. Your organization makes you successful, not some kind of fairy tale super leader. How can you make your venture teams successful? What do they need to move forward? Where do organizational anti-dotes pop up?

Change

There is a lot of talk about change. Some say we need to be inspired or motivated to change. Others believe it is all about authenticity, whatever that means. We cannot inspire people to become great, that is the results of the habits people have, how they think and behave, on a daily basis. Habits will lead you where they take you, intentions not. Now why do people change? Two reasons, because they can (competence) and because it is necessary (urgency). Now why is mediocrity then more contagious than excellence?

Maybe as Lee Thayer says: "Most people prefer a problem they can't solve above a solution they don't like".

In many organizations, mistakes start at the day-to-day level. How people communicate with each other and whether they communicate. How people avoid tensions or conflicts with colleagues or not. They fix somebody else's problem or complain about it to other people. When nobody understands who is accountable for what, you have the beginning of mediocre performance.

To create new waves of growth and prosperity for everyone, we need to be bold and lead the way. The leaders of our companies should be aware that they don't need to be the superhero leader who fixes everything, they should take care of their people and their mindset and habits of working. If you create the right conditions and ways of working, the organization makes the leader successful. This is challenging work. People say they want to learn or change, but they'd prefer to see other people change (first). It's tough to accept that moving from the present situation to the desired situation is difficult and will take time. The point is that if we act as if we are in the desired situation, we are already 80% there.

I strongly believe that it is necessary to reinvent our companies and ourselves, and it is our moral obligation to create new waves of growth for our future generations. Don't take this subject lightly, give (disruptive) innovation in all its aspects the senior leadership attention and appropriate funding to move beyond a *tick in the box*, to real business impact.

A big thanks to all the great people that I have met in my life, that formed me as a person, my thinking and essentially who I am. My wife for being the cornerstone of our family and giving me the space to create my destiny. I'm forever grateful. My children, the ones for whom I want to become a better person.

All the great thinkers Lee Thayer, Clayton Christensen, Steve Blank and many others. My great colleagues from Innoleaps, especially Jeroen Tjepkema, who provided me with fresh perspectives and enriched the chapter about venture building. I am standing on the shoulders of giants.

I wish you a great and bumpy journey!

Misha de Sterke

Notes

Chapter 1 Corporate innovation – an introduction

1   Stadler, Christian 2010, *Enduring Success*, Stanford Business Books

2   Innosight, 2017

3   Farrell, John 2018, KPMG Benchmark Innovation Impact 2018: https://info.kpmg.us/innovation-and-enterprise-solutions/ benchmarking-innovation-impact-2018.html

4   Buck, Raphael, Alex Harper, Julie Lowrie, and Sara Prince 2019, Agile in the consumer goods industry: https://www.mckinsey.com/ business-functions/marketing-and-sales/our-insights/agile-in-the- consumer-goods-industry-the-transformation-of-the-brand-manager

5   Predictive Consumer Growth 2013-2017, MckInsey

6   Wolcott, Robert C. https://www.forbes.com/sites/robertwolcott/ 2019/03/15/kraft-heinz-route-to-ruin-or-revival-3g-capital-its-time- for-courage/#7b3d4d9d44bc

7   Foster, Richard and Sarah Kaplan 2001, *Creative Destruction*, Currency

8   Thayer, Lee 2016, The leader's journey (blog)

9   Foster, Richard and Sarah Kaplan 2001, *Creative Destruction*, Currency

10 Tushman, Michael L. and Charles A. O'Reilly III 2016, *Lead and Disrupt*, Stanford Business Books

11 Mattes, Frank and Ralph-Christian Ohr 2018, *Scaling-up Corporate Startups*

Chapter 2 The 10x Growth Machine system

[11] Gruber, Marc and Sharon Tal 2018, *Where to Play*, Financial Times Publishing

[12] Osterwalder, Alexander and Yves Pigneur (2010) *Business Model Generation*, Wiley

[14] Croll, Alistair and Benjamin Yoskovitz 2013, *Lean Analytics*, O'Reilly

Chapter 3 Growth Strategy and Portfolio management

[15] Ulwick, Anthony W. and Alexander Osterwalder 2016, *Jobs to be Done*, IDEA Bite Press

[16] Christensen, Clayton M. and Michael E. Raynor 2013, *The Innovator's Solution*, Harvard Business Review Press

[17] Christensen, Clayton M. and Michael E. Raynor 2013, *The Innovator's Solution*, Harvard Business Review Press

[18] Argyris, Chris 1977, Double loop learning in organizations, Harvard Business Review: https://hbr.org/1977/09/double-loop-learning-in-organizations

[19] SMAC and DARQ abbreviations: Accenture's Technology Vision 2019

[20] Foster, Richard and Sarah Kaplan 2001, *Creative Destruction*, Currency

[21] Blank, Steve and Bob Dorf 2013, *The Startup Owner's Manual*, K&S Ranch

[22] Venkatraman, Vik 2019, *Mechanized: Nearly automated, nearly monkey- proof, new product innovation methodology*

Chapter 4 Corporate Venture Building

Chapter 4 was co-authored by Jeroen Tjepkema and we're thankful for his assistance.

[23] Ulwick, Anthony W. and Alexander Osterwalder 2016, *Jobs to be Done*, IDEA Bite Press

[24] IDC Manufacturing Insights

[25] McClure, Dave 2007, Pirate Metrics, article on Medium.com

Chapter 5 Growth accounting

[26] This is an excerpt from the work of *Robert C. Wolcott and Michael J. Lippitz*, 2007 The Four Models of Corporate Entrepreneurship: https://sloanreview.mit.edu/article/the-four-models-of-corporate-entrepreneurship

[27] Blank, Steve and Bob Dorf 2013, *The Startup Owner's Manual*, K&S Ranch

[28] Based on the work of Steve Blank

[29] Mattes, Frank and Ralph-Christian Ohr 2018, *Scaling-up Corporate Startups*

Afterword

[30] Schneider, Joan and Julie Hall, https://hbr.org/2011/04/why-most-product-launches-fail

[31] Farrell, John 2018, KPMG Benchmark Innovation Impact 2018: https://info.kpmg.us/innovation-and-enterprise-solutions/benchmarking-innovation-impact-2018.html

Literature

Accenture's Technology Vision 2019

Anthony, Scott D., S. Patrick Viguerie, Evan I. Schwartz and John Van Landeghem 2018, Corporate Longevity Forecast 2018: https://www.innosight.com/wp-content/uploads/2017/11/Innosight-Corporate-Longevity-2018.pdf

Argyris, Chris 1977, Double loop learning in organizations, Harvard Business Review: https://hbr.org/1977/09/double-loop-learning-in-organizations

Blank, Steve 2013, *The Four Steps to the Epiphany*, K&S Ranch

Blank, Steve, blogs at www.steveblank.com

Buck, Raphael, Alex Harper, Julie Lowrie, and Sara Prince 2019, Agile in the consumer goods industry: https://www.mckinsey.com/business-functions/marketing-and-sales/our-insights/agile-in-the-consumer-goods-industry-the-transformation-of-the-brand-manager

Croll, Alistair and Benjamin Yoskovitz 2013, *Lean Analytics*, O'Reilly

Christensen, Clayton M. and Michael E. Raynor 2013, *The Innovator's Solution*, Harvard Business Review Press

Christensen, Clayton M. 2016, *The Innovator's Dilemma*, Harvard Business Review Press

Dan, Avi 2019, The Lesson of The Kraft Heinz Nosedive, at Forbes.com: https://www.forbes.com/sites/avidan/2019/02/24/the-lesson-of-the-kraft-heinz-nosedive-radical-cost-cutting-is-out-brands-are-back

Dunford, April 2019, *Obviously Awesome*, Ambient Press

Farrell, John 2018, KPMG Benchmark Innovation Impact 2018: https://info.kpmg.us/innovation-and-enterprise-solutions/benchmarking-innovation-impact-2018.html

Foster, Richard and Sarah Kaplan 2001, *Creative Destruction*, Currency

McClure, Dave 2007, Pirate Metrics, article on Medium.com

McKinsey Predictive Consumer Growth, 2013-2017

Ohr, Ralph-Christian, blogs at www.integrative-innovation.net

Tushman, Michael L. and Charles A. O'Reilly III 2016, *Lead and Disrupt*, Stanford Business Books

Osterwalder, Alexander and Yves Pigneur 2010, *Business model Generation*, Wiley

Osterwalder, Alexander and Yves Pigneur, et al 2014, *Value Proposition Design*, Wiley

Ries, Eric 2017, *The Startup Way*, Currency

Stadler, Christian 2010, *Enduring Success*, Stanford Business Books

Thayer, Lee, blogs at www.thethayerinsitute.org

Ulwick, Anthony W. and Alexander Osterwalder 2016, *Jobs to be Done*, IDEA Bite Press

Wolcott, Robert C. and Michael J. Lippitz 2007, The Four Models of Corporate Entrepreneurship: https://sloanreview.mit.edu/article/the-four-models-of-corporate-entrepreneurship

About the Author

Misha de Sterke is a corporate innovation and startup expert and has extensive experience. In the corporate world as an interim manager and staff advisor on digital transformation, and as an entrepreneur building different tech-driven startups.

He works for numerous Fortune 100 companies on disruptive strategy and venture building, focussing on achieving growth. He advises C-level executives on how to build the 10X Growth Machine and he coaches startups on turning ideas into profitable businesses. He also lectures at several Dutch universities about entrepreneurship and innovation and has a special interest in managing irrationality and tension in teams to forge bold outcomes.

He is currently leading a corporate innovation practice that operates on a global scale.